AMBER SWENOR

Unleashed

A BEEN-THERE, ROCKED-THAT GUIDE TO

Radical Authenticity

IN LIFE AND BUSINESS

WORLDCHANGERS
MEDIA

Hardcover: 978-1-955811-17-0
Paperback: 978-1-955811-03-3
E-book: 978-1-955811-09-5
LCCN: 2021925250

First hardcover edition: April 2022

Edited by Bryna Haynes / www.WorldChangers.media
Cover design by Mila / www.milagraphicartist.com/
Layout & interior by Paul Baillie-Lane / www.pblpublishing.co.uk
Cover Photo by Kate Fore / www.kateforeboudoir.com

Published by WorldChangers Media
PO Box 83, Foster, RI 02825
www.WorldChangers.Media

Disclaimer

This book is dedicated to ...
Every visionary who dreamed "too big."
Every heart-centered, sensitive soul who felt like "too much," and felt "too much."
Everyone who didn't fit the mold.
You are exactly who you are meant to be, and who you are becoming.
You need you. The world needs you.
Here's to becoming fully Unleashed.

PEOPLE ARE SAYING . . .

"Now more than ever, we need women like Amber—women with bold ideas and strong, unique voices, who aren't afraid to use them to change the world. Luckily for us, in *Unleashed*, Amber walks us through the steps everyone can take to become one of those change-makers, and sets us on the path to leadership, authenticity, and transformation. Raw and honest, compassionate yet no-nonsense, painfully relatable and often hilarious, *Unleashed* doesn't pull its punches: Amber speaks the truth even when it hurts, and teaches us how to speak ours."

Alyse Nelson
President and CEO, Vital Voices Global Partnership

"Most of us spend our lives trying not to be, or look, selfish. In *Unleashed*, Amber helps us to understand why prioritizing who we are is actually a gift to everybody. In these pages she not only inspires us to move past our limits to self-expression, but provides practical tools to do so. *Unleashed* is a journey worth taking!"

Darla LeDoux
Coach, Trainer and Founder of Sourced

"*Unleashed* gives you the permission (and the blueprint) to turn up the dial on the most authentic soul version of exactly WHO you truly are ... and WHO the world needs right now for this next shift."

Yanik Silver
Creator of *The Cosmic Journal*
and author of *Evolved Enterprise*

"The future is for rebels, and *Unleashed* is the manifesto for authentic, positive change. This book is not just a play-by-play on how you can 'get' more in your life; rather, it showcases Amber's unconventional, inspirational story of how you can BE more of yourself naturally, and leverage that to attract aligned opportunities, clients, and prosperity. Through her embodiment of authenticity, Amber inspires others to embrace the aspects of themselves that don't fit neatly into the box of the status quo, and pioneers a pathway for deeper meaning in what historically has been full of hollow pursuit."

Makhosi Nejeser
The Royal Shaman

"Amber is a powerful mirror who helps others recognize their truth, authenticity, and potential. Her power is shining a light on others, guiding them to the fullest expression of their authentic self, and *Unleashed* is the product of that power—giving readers the ability to awaken their authentic selves so they can go out and live their epic missions while creating a ripple effect that transforms the world! This book will show you that authenticity is an inside job, one that you're ready to harness and use, to create massive joy and success."

Meghann Conter
Founder and Chief Laugh Instigator, The Dames

"All my life I have been attracted to left-of-center people—people who strive to be authentic, who follow their own drumbeat, who are non-conformists and disruptors, and who have a genuineness about them that just draws you in. Amber is that person. She exemplifies a badass woman through her appearance and self-expression. And, in *Unleashed,* she weaves you into what created the incredible authenticity in which she lives her life and runs her business. You will be inspired to look at your own life, permissioned to find your own drumbeat, and encouraged to be truly authentic. Not your average self-help/business book, *Unleashed* is a book to kickstart your audacious journey and find your inner badass along the way."

Christie Bemis
Psychotherapist, Author, Speaker,
Sex Educator & Relationship Coach

"For every woman who's been told not to rock the boat, not to color outside the lines, or that they need to conform to expectations ... it's time to unleash your inner badass. In *Unleashed*, Amber shows you how to do that with inspiring stories, real life examples, and practical tools. In a world where we're starved for real voices and inundated with people pretending to have all the answers, we now have an authentic voice to inspire us to release our fears, trust our decisions, and show up fully. *Unleashed* gives you a peek into what it looks like to take calculated risks that are empowered by intuition, and shows us how trusting yourself and making bold moves actually does pay off. Amber's stories are transparent, never sugarcoated, and are presented as jumping-off points for your own authenticity, joy, and business success."

Emily Bissen
Founder & Business Development Coach, Blue Heron Business Partners

"An honest, vulnerable, glitter bomb of inspiration! *Unleashed* makes you want to jump up and embrace your badass self immediately. After Amber's energy enters your life, her spark will ignite you to reach higher, dream bigger, and redefine success in every aspect of your life. If you're ready to listen to that deep, soulful knowing that you have been 'playing it safe,' Amber will embrace you, guide you, and provide you with solid, actionable strategies to shed limiting fears and unleash your whole self. Amber is a rockstar sage whose wisdom inspires you to believe that your dreams are within reach."

Katie Hill
Founder and Chief Rebel, Rebel Wellness

"As we grow as leaders, we are constantly hearing messages about the right way to lead, or to act, or to be in professional settings. We internalize these messages, and it can be hard to separate them from our own internal compass of what we know to be the right way for ourselves. *Unleashed* is an amazing tool to take a step back and reflect on our own truth, to build our own authentic path forward. When I think of the most genuine, true-to-herself, unapologetic leader I know, I think of Amber Swenor. She is absolutely unique and shines in her authentic self because she's done the work to quiet the other voices in her head and lead from the heart. This book is a wonderful exploration of her own journey, and also gives the reader the tools to unleash their own badass, authentic self."

Maddy Niebauer, CEO & Founder, vChief

"Amber's story is one that most of us can see ourselves in: having a desire to be our true selves, but feeling conflicted about how our true self might be at odds with those around us. Her vulnerability and candidness are refreshing and encouraging. A heavy metal frontwoman who is able to connect with people on a spiritual and energetic level isn't something you come across in the coaching or self-help world. While other books will tell you to change your mindset, or, 'Go wash your face and journal,' Amber actually walks the walk and gives us the tools to do the same if we are ready to become fully Unleashed. We root for her throughout her journey because when we are rooting for her, we are rooting for ourselves."

Melissa DaSilva
Life Coach, Artist, Founder of East Coast Mental Wellness

"Amber knows her stuff and is willing to share everything about her journey to finding her most authentic self so you can use Unleashed as a tool to unlock the best version of you. *Unleashed* is a book for every entrepreneur, leader, and human being to add to their bookshelf to achieve the life of their dreams. Amber is a great example of what happens when you show up, do the work, and push every day to be better!"

Chris Winfield
COO, Super Connector Media

TABLE OF CONTENTS

INTRODUCTION

"A heart-centered metalhead business strategist is a thing, and you're about to meet her!"

That's my favorite way to introduce myself of late. And yet, it wasn't too long ago that announcing myself to a new group of people this way would make make me question if I was "too much." For years, people saw me as "the girl who marches to her own drum"—and I was. But also, I wasn't.

I still worried about what everyone thought. I still agonized over how much the *true* me wanted to rock like crazy onstage, dye her hair funky colors, and get visible tattoos, while at the same time battling the "professional" me who wanted to be taken seriously. The result was that I toned down every part of my expression. Sure, I was marching to my own drum, but I was still keeping someone else's beat.

So many people I know do some version of this. But it begs the question: if fitting into your chosen world requires you to suppress every part of you that you know to be authentic and true, why the fuck would you want to be part of that world?

Over the last several years, I've decided that to be a part of a world in which we all belong requires that we make it so. Thankfully, there are thousands, maybe even millions, of others who are deciding to do their part to make this world one in which we all belong. You've picked up this book because you are one of them.

I've been a rockstar from birth (as you'll come to see), but that doesn't mean this book is only for rockers. I'm a rockstar because that is the most authentic expression of my soul. Maybe yours is different—maybe your most authentic self is a librarian, or a folk singer, or a fighter jet pilot. The expression is your own. But the energy is the same.

You've picked up this book because you understand, deep in your soul, that it's time to be *all of you.* And you're not willing to spend *one more moment* squeezing yourself into a box that can no longer contain you. You're not only ready to march to your own drum; you want to rock on your own damn *stage.*

You are ready to live Unleashed.

TURN UP THE VOLUME

As a kid, I was the "academic goth" who wore seven-inch glitter platforms to Quiz Bowl, rocked pleather pants to show pigs at the county fair, and curled my hair with loads of hairspray to play softball. But as an empath susceptible to shame and its conditioning, I struggled.

Externally, I was the life of the party. Internally, I constantly battled self-doubt.

Externally, I shone on stages as a public speaker—and, later, as a singer. Internally, I was drowning in shame and guilt for "outshining" those around me.

This is the dichotomy faced by those of us who are unwilling to settle for anything less than radical authenticity. We love the world, and the people in it—and yet, living in a way that values them while *also* valuing ourselves can feel impossible.

I promise you, it's not.

But valuing yourself *must* come first. And that's the essence of what I'm going to teach you in this book.

Since making my decision to honor my authenticity and follow my soul's guidance in life and business—and in helping hundreds of clients to do the same—I've learned that becoming Unleashed is a multi-step process. It requires you to Uncover your truth and understand it on a soul level. Then, you can Unlock the guiding principles and core values that form the foundation of your most radically authentic life. Then, finally, you can Unleash your truest self in all aspects of your life in a clear, supported, and radically badass way.

But before you can do any of that ... you need to make a decision.

So, let me ask you ...

Can you *choose*, here and now, to no longer play small?

Can you *choose* your authentic self over others' beliefs, desires, and expectations—even if you don't know what that looks like yet?

Can you *choose* to walk a path that's never been traveled before, and that might at times be challenging or even scary, because it's been waiting for *you*?

If you're hesitant to make that choice, my suggestion is that you put this book down and come back when you're ready to make that massive commitment. Because until you fully say "Yes!" to yourself and do what it takes to become Unleashed, everything you're about to learn will be just ... theory.

As you'll learn in these pages, knowing and doing are not the same thing.

THE WORLD NEEDS YOU

The truth is, the world will never be "ready" for you as your most Unleashed self. And yet, the world *needs* that version of you, and it needs you now.

When you Unleash yourself, you carve a space in the world that is all your own. You become a beacon of light in a dark maze of expectations, "norms," and tired tropes. You no longer need to shift how you act, what you say, or what you believe to fit in. You no longer need to pretend to make others comfortable.

But, most of all, you no longer need others to do those things to share space with you. By becoming Unleashed, you make space for others to Unleash themselves.

That, my friend, is a truly awesome thing.

So on that note ... let's begin.

PART 1

UNCOVER

CHAPTER 1

STRIPPING IT BARE

There are three truths in my life that have been with me for as long as I can remember

Dogs. Africa. Rock-N-Roll.

Dogs are an easy one to understand. I love them. They love me. They teach me to slow down, appreciate the moment, and get off my damn phone once in a while.

Africa was always with me, even before I knew where (or what) Africa was. I knew I'd go there someday, even if it wasn't clear why.

But rock-n-roll ... that was my *soul*.

From the time I could dress myself, I opted for anything mismatched, glittery, jangly, or leather. The weirder, the better—because I was a *rock superstar*, and everybody knows that rock superstars have their very own look.

Only Madonna is Madonna. Only Joan Jett can be Joan Jett. Only Cyndi is Cyndi. And only I was Amber. Didn't matter that "Amber" was one of the top baby names of the 80s. I was *Thee* Amber.

In hindsight, it's obvious that I was born a rebel.

But, although my superstardom has felt like a core truth since I was a kid, I haven't always lived it. Somewhere along the way, something dulled my shine, quieted the rebellion, and forced me into a watered-down, backstage role in my own story.

As a young teenager, I realized that lowering my volume was the best way to be accepted. I still kind of danced to my own beat, and other people perceived me as unique and authentic—but I knew I was only 20 percent of the way there.

If you can imagine your insides feeling like a rocket ship, all revved up and ready for blastoff ... but you just sit there on the launch pad with fumes billowing all around you, feeling like you're about to combust if you can't just explode into the sky already and show them what you're made of ...

Yeah, that was how I felt for most of my twenties. I knew I was just scratching the surface of my truth. I knew I was selling myself short. I yearned to show up fully and confidently, as all of me. But I had no idea how to do it.

Maybe this is you, too.

Maybe you were born to be larger than life, but your experiences have left you with crippling self-doubt. Maybe you find yourself thinking, "People already think I'm too loud, too weird, too bold. They already think I make 'bad' choices. What are they going to say if I go all the way?"

In this world, being the star of your own life can feel *hard*—especially if you're authentically a rebel. People don't want you to be so ... big. "Larger than life" pushes *all* the buttons for people who've spent their lives trying to fit into other people's boxes. They'd rather see you fall off the stage than give you a standing ovation. What's worse, they actually think they're *protecting* you by asking you to stay small.

But here's the thing: if you do the work to uncover your authenticity, you'll get to a point where it actually becomes easier to be you than to keep pretending to be someone else. When people you care about walk out of the auditorium, you'll find the strength to keep playing.

And the people who stick around? They're your true friends, and your true fans. They'll cheer their hearts out, and sing along while you belt out a truth from your soul.

They'll echo the sound of your truth back to you—and you will do the same for them.

Your desires are epic. Freedom is your anthem. And that internal combustion? It's going to propel your glitter-dusted, rainbow-mohawked self into orbit, attract your dream clients and soul family, and fully unleash the one and only *you* into the world.

Thee you. The you who needs no introduction.

AUTHENTICITY IS NOT A BUZZWORD

As a business coach, particularly coaching many women for years, I've seen some core patterns and fears that seem to show up consistently for heart-centered rebels. In our work together, my clients—an amazing group of creatives, coaches, healers, and service providers—have frequently asked questions like ...

- "Is it really safe to be *all* of me?"
- "If I walk into a room as my confident, badass self, will others resent me?
- "If I stop trying to make other people comfortable, what does that say about me?"
- "Am I actually smart enough to be a leader?"
- "If I hold my boundaries, will that make me a bitch?"
- "If I want to earn more than what I need to survive, does that make me greedy?"

And, most of all …

- "Who the hell am I to have this big dream?"

In every case, the inner narrative is the same:

- "Don't shine too brightly or you'll get burned."
- "Don't be too bold. You'll make people want to hurt you."
- "I need to be responsible for everyone."
- "You don't deserve to have it all."

As I worked with women across all stages and levels of business, it became clear to me that the one ingredient necessary to success in any venture isn't a marketing strategy, a brand identity, or even a killer product. Our direct link to success is *how we perceive ourselves and how we show up in the world.*

In other words, claiming our unmistakable rockstar identity and embracing our authenticity is the key to creating everything we desire. The rest is just details.

Since I had this realization, I've been committed to helping other heart-centered visionaries create businesses that are truly aligned with their authentic selves and that support their dreams and desires. Yes, we delve into strategic, actionable steps along the way (many of which I'll be sharing with you in this book), but the real work starts from within. This is a journey of fully uncovering, understanding, and unleashing the most badass, rebellious, potent version of you, and coming to feel a sense of total peace, pride, and power in who you are.

The word "authenticity" may be overused lately, but that doesn't mean it's a hollow concept. To live authentically is one of the bravest, most rebel-icious things you can do. It's the opposite of self-serving. It's *freedom*-serving—for you, and for everyone around you.

Why? Because you can't change the world until you're ready to take the stage.

Maybe you're reading this and thinking, "Oh, crap. I'm not ready for this!" You're not alone in that feeling, and you're also more than ready. The fact that you're reading this book is proof that you've put your feet on the path. If this is you, hang in there, because your rocket-launch countdown is starting. Think of me as a star in your sky—someone who has been there, done that, and lived to shout it across the Universe—and who is still learning, every day, how *not* to dim her light.

Or, maybe you're in a different place with your rebel-licious self. Maybe you're saying, "I know I'm a rebel. I was born that way. So *what*, exactly, do I need help with?"

If that's you, I have to ask: Are you showing up as the most badass version of you in *all* the places, relationships, and situations in your life? Or are you still censoring yourself at the office, with your significant other, or with your friends or family? Are you living a double life, only revealing the true you to the most forgiving audience? Is there *more* that's possible for you, if you could just allow yourself to let loose?

If the answer is no ... well, badass, I salute you. But if you're anything like me, you still have some barriers that need stripping away.

That's the work we'll be doing together in this book.

WE ARE TAUGHT TO HIDE WHO WE ARE

As you may have guessed, I've always been strong-willed.

As *Thee* Amber, I wore what I wanted, said what I wanted, and did what I wanted. It didn't matter to me that Reeboks were the latest fashion; I was all about my fuzzy moccasins and puffy neon coat. And, of course, big-ass headphones were my primary accessory. I moved through the world as if I owned it, and I asked *lots* of questions.

At five, six, and seven years old, I sang at the top of my lungs. I let my tummy hang out. I used my body as an instrument of freedom as I danced, played, and ran. I pretended to be a dog getting into a big kennel, and my cousins found a creative way to feed me chips through the fence—right until my horrified aunt ran up, screaming, "Why is she eating out of the pooper-scooper?"

I wasn't worried about what other people thought of me. I was the boss of my world, and that was exactly how I liked it because it felt like how it was "supposed" to be.

But as I got older, I started to notice that this behavior was becoming less and less amusing to the adults around me. Instead of calling me "cute," they were acting judgmental and pissy—as if my confidence and directness were somehow threatening to them. My uncles started making comments like, "You ask a lot of questions," or, "Shouldn't you be playing with your Barbie dolls or something?" which implied that my presence was only tolerable to them while they found it amusing, and that I should otherwise shut up and stay out of the way. My parents, totally unprepared for a child who had no intention of rule-following, brushed me off when I asked questions about things like gender roles or societal norms, likely because they themselves didn't have the answers.

Bit by bit, my glitter was stripped. My shine was covered up.

It wasn't one thing: it was everything. Negative feedback from the people around me. Confusing descriptions of my body and what it meant to the world (i.e. being referred to as "Amber with the big boobs," as if my boobs were the only valuable thing about me). Stereotypical descriptions of starving artists and deadbeat musicians in movies and TV shows. The message that "if you're not as big as Beyonce, don't bother." Consequences for women who said too much, too loudly. Internal anguish about desiring my family's love and support, while struggling with the fact that my mere existence threatened their comfort zones, and even their whole way of life.

Despite some pretty crazy moments, when I look back, it wasn't any one person, event, or situation that took the proverbial microphone out of my hands. It was a cumulative effect—my personal circumstances blended with the consequences of growing up in a society that simultaneously values uniqueness and devalues authenticity. These layers of programming and perspective needed to be uncovered, understood, and healed before *Thee* Amber could finally be Unleashed.

"ARE YOU SHOWING UP AS THE MOST BADASS VERSION OF YOU IN ALL THE PLACES, RELATIONSHIPS, AND SITUATIONS IN YOUR LIFE?"

The same goes for you, my friend.

Uncovering who we truly are requires looking at *why* we are the way we are. Looking at the parts that make us feel lit up and alive in a positive way, as well as the parts that make us feel shame, frustration, or rage. We all have light and shadow within us; only by understanding and embracing both can we truly feel whole.

It's important to explain here that, while many people who are shamed out of their rockstar personas may (rightfully) blame their upbringing, their parents, or society, we are all ultimately responsible for initiating any healing or forgiveness that may be needed in the process of claiming our truth. It's true that many of the most challenging parts of my journey were the result of the conditioning, poor decisions, and painful outcomes experienced and perpetuated through generations in my family—but I also know that everyone did the best they could with what they had, and in the case of my immediate upbringing, my parents did better for us than the generation before. Blaming my upbringing for my struggles may have been a reasonable excuse for a while, but that didn't get me closer to becoming my true self or getting to where I wanted to go.

Recognizing what isn't mine to hold onto has been a continuous unfolding. This has become possible for me because of my commitment to personal truth and authenticity. Until I reached a place where I could make—and vocalize—that commitment, I couldn't step out of the shadows and do the deeper work around my life experiences and trauma.

So, if you have past experiences, traumas, or conditioning that is standing between you and who you feel you are truly meant to become, please seek out resources to help you understand it in a way that is healthy and aligned for you. Let the work we do together be a catalyst for your greater alignment, where all the parts of who you are and what you've experienced become useful pieces of information. At the same time, understand that what we do together will be part of a greater network of guidance and support that you create for yourself along your journey—because, hey, every rockstar needs an entourage!

YOUR PERSONAL TRUTH IS YOUR PATH TO FREEDOM

Everyone and their mother has an opinion.

Sometimes, those opinions float by like music from a distant car stereo. And sometimes, they echo in your ears for years.

I've heard some whoppers in my life. Some of them I laughed off. Others I internalized; they became hidden commitments I had to overcome. They became head games I played with myself until I finally woke up to the fact that they weren't true and *they didn't belong to me*.

Your personal truth is your path to freedom. But your personal truth is your naked skin. Sometimes, you have to strip away layer after layer of fabrics and shapes that were stitched by other people in order to actually see who you are.

I like to think of the untruths we absorb as "rags." They're not the things *you* choose to express and adorn your authentic self with. They're other people's cast-off junk that you just happened to pick up and think, "It kinda fits, so I guess I should keep it."

Some of my "rags" have included thoughts like:

- You can't be powerful and soft-hearted at the same time.
- You can't be an artist and be taken seriously in business.
- You can't be competitive and driven, because then you're a bitch.
- You can't be emotional and loving, because then you're weak.
- You can't be too successful, because then your family will think you're stuck-up.

When I decided to strip down and get real about what was mine, I realized that *none* of these were true.

In this book, I'm going to help you learn to navigate the fears of judgment, abandonment, and "rocking the boat" that are keeping these head games alive for you. This includes the judgments you put on yourself. I don't have a magic pill that will wipe out all the layers of "rags" you've been hiding under—but I do have the tools to get you started on this journey, and the experience to help you use them. Your shine is too damn important to be held back by lies and fears.

We'll talk about this in a lot more depth later in the book, but for now, I want you to realize that you will never find freedom while you are still hiding under the "rags" others have handed you. Your joy, your freedom, and your utter stardom are natural consequences of your authenticity. You want these things for a reason. You don't have to explain or justify your desires to anyone. The fact that you feel them is enough. In fact, it's cluing you in to the fact that you're onto something *big*.

When you become ready to strip down, shake off the rags, and get vulnerable, you will realize something profound: When you put down those judgments and "shoulds," you have nothing left to lose. When you take away the stuff others have handed you and expected you to wear, you have nothing left to fear—and only freedom to gain.

Your experiences thus far in life were your chrysalis; they created a space for you to take form. But when the time comes, you need to be ready to crack that cozy, safe shell and leave them behind. If you don't climb out and spread your wings, sooner or later, you'll wither.

You didn't come here for a half-formed life. You came here for the whole damn thing.

Are you ready to claim it?

Me too.

So fluff up your hair, put on your cut-offs (or your couture gown, if that's what tickles your fancy), because it's time to clear the clouds on the *you* who has always been there.

"YOUR SHINE
IS TOO DAMN
IMPORTANT TO
BE HELD BACK BY
LIES AND FEARS."

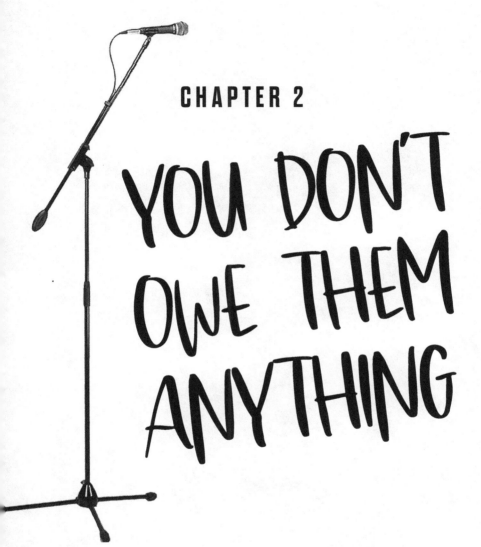

CHAPTER 2

YOU DON'T OWE THEM ANYTHING

was five years old. My mother and I were sitting in the office of my family doctor.

I liked this doctor; he seemed to be a genuinely nice guy. I also noticed that the adults in the room—my mother, the medical assistant, the nurses—perked up whenever he walked in. In fact, my mom's mood would shift perceptibly when he greeted her.

Growing up, there was a lot of stress and arguing in my household, often centered around money. My parents worked long, hard hours to make ends meet, but there never seemed to be enough to keep up with car repairs, expenses, medical bills ...

Even at five years old, I understood that everything required money. Even this doctor's visit. And yet, despite the fact that paying for this appointment would probably mean there wasn't enough money to go around elsewhere, my mom seemed happier in the room with this doctor, and I took note.

I asked, "How did you become a doctor?"

"I went to college to learn how to practice medicine," he replied with a smile.

By this age, I had an understanding that things cost money, so of course my next question was, "How did you pay for that?"

He didn't miss a beat. "I worked really hard. I graduated as valedictorian, and got scholarships that helped pay for college."

It didn't take my five-year-old mind long to connect the dots.

Work hard = valedictorian (whatever that was)

Valedictorian = college

College = become a doctor

Become a doctor = Mom is happy! No more fighting!

From that moment, I proclaimed I would be valedictorian and go to college.

I talked about college from that point forward, but my parents didn't say much in reply. They didn't understand my newfound drive. Neither my parents, nor their parents or their siblings, had finished high school, let alone attended university. I'm sure they also felt some level of self-doubt about their lack of understanding about the college process, and stress about how to pay for it. But I was determined.

By the time I was seventeen, I was indeed ranked first in my high school class. As I started looking into colleges, it became clear that, despite my hard work, being valedictorian wasn't going to be enough to get the scholarships needed to cover the full tuition.

I told my mom about my conundrum—but my mind wasn't changed. "I'm going to college," I told her stubbornly.

She responded anxiously, "Oh, Amber. *People like us don't go to college.*"

This hurt. Not because my mom didn't believe in me, because on one level, she did. But it hurt deeply because like many things in life, I knew I would be walking this journey alone.

I knew exactly who "people like us" were. However, my mind was made up. While I shared some of the same conditioning, her fear wasn't mine, and I wasn't going to let anything stop me.

"Mom, I understand we don't have the money. I'm not asking you to pay for it. I'm going to get loans. And it's going to be worth it."

Whenever I'm tempted to listen to people who say, "You can't," I remember that moment. At seventeen, I chose to trust my truth, and my path. My determination to make a choice for myself, despite everything that was pre-determined around me, was the first step in breaking the chains of poverty and fear.

So often we're told what we can and cannot be, what we can and cannot do. These aren't truths; they're limiting beliefs. Nevertheless, they run deep. And they can affect us in ways we don't anticipate, long after we make the choice to supersede them.

A few months after that conversation with my mom, I graduated as valedictorian of my class, becoming only the second person in my family to earn a high school diploma (after my sister), and the first to be accepted to and attend college.

Standing there, in front of my family, my school friends, and our small farming community, I delivered my speech in seven-inch, bright red glittery platforms and two-toned hair. I was the goth-farm-girl who had broken all the rules.

That day remains one of my proudest rebel moments. In that moment, on that stage, I stepped into my own shine, and shot my star a little higher into the cosmos.

WHY DO WE PLAY BY *THEIR* RULES?

You're here because you're being called into a more authentic, badass, hyper-aligned vision for yourself. You're here because you belong here, on this planet, at this time—but you're not here to fit in with the masses. That's not what "belonging" means. In fact, you're here to break all the rules—and have fun doing it.

If you ever decide that you do, in fact, want rules, you can write them yourself. Because the rules you write yourself are the only rules that matter.

That's what it means to live Unleashed.

No matter what the people around you say, playing by others' rules is a choice. It doesn't matter what anyone around you thinks or feels about your dreams. It doesn't matter what your family did before you. It doesn't matter what you've had to overcome, what shame stories you're carrying, or what resources you have (or don't have) in this moment.

You always have the choice to be all of you, *right now.*

That's what "people like us" do. That's what we choose, every day.

As Unleashed beings, we put ourselves in situations where we know we're going to get uncomfortable, so we can break out of the box and get to where we want to go. Then, once we get comfortable in that new skin, we'll probably do it all again. The Unleashed path is about paving the road to our authenticity, walking it bravely, and coming back home to our truest selves at the end of it all.

"TO FULLY UNLEASH YOUR TRUTH, YOU HAVE TO BE WILLING TO BECOME THAT IDEAL YOU'RE SEARCHING FOR."

Living Unleashed might mean breaking the only bonds you've ever known. That's what it meant for me. I wasn't just following my dreams. I was cracking the stone walls of poverty, under-education, abuse, fear, and self-minimizing that had defined my family's reality for generations.

When I work with clients around this, we start by looking at their unique "rules for living"—the values that feel most authentic to them. Once we know the rules they want to follow—the rules they wrote—we can see exactly why and how all the bullshit rules of "what's been done" and "what's expected" don't line up with what they are choosing for themselves.

DECLARING YOURSELF IS ONLY THE FIRST STEP

My valedictorian speech was my declaration that my primary Rule for Living no longer matched what I'd grown up with. *Woo-hoo! Superstardom, here I come!*

However, living into this new vision—and living up to my own expectations for it—wasn't so easy.

Part of my strategy for making *Thee* Amber acceptable in my little farm town was to live in half-truths. I had the ability to fit in with almost any group. Geeks, farm kids, goths, and athletes: I was friends with, and fit in with, all of them. But in every group, I hid parts of my truest self. With my FFA friends (that's formerly Future Farmers of

America, for those not familiar), I toned down my wild hair and makeup and didn't talk about my dreams of being the frontwoman in a metal band. With my goth-rocker friends, I kept my scholarly goals to myself. With the athletes, I left my platform heels at home, and let my abilities—or lack thereof—speak for themselves; one benefit of being from a small town is that everyone makes the team.

Today, this behavior is known as "code-shifting"—the act of changing who you are to better fit in. Back then, I just thought of it as survival. The truth was, I was *terrified* of not being liked. I was bold, but also super sensitive. I'd cry for days if someone said something bad about me. And even if, after a glance through my high school yearbooks, one would argue that there was no fitting in for Amber—with my two-toned hair and sparkly pleather pants—I knew, deep down, exactly how much I was holding back.

I was literally the meekest, least offensive "rebel" on the planet.

FFA was one of the hardest places for me, because even though I deeply respected my FFA advisor, Mr. A., loved the program and my friends there, and it afforded me opportunities to learn and grow, the expectations for what was "proper" were constrictive. While I was winning speaking competitions, going to nationals, and leading youth leadership workshops as a state FFA officer, I felt like the true me was being totally rejected. The whole organization was contradictory to my values around self-expression and authenticity. Even when we were allowed to trade our (very conservative) uniforms—corduroy jackets, black skirts, closed-toe black pumps that looked like they should belong to my grandmother—for "normal" clothes, we couldn't wear tank tops or sandals, never mind pleather and platforms. Everything was constructed to preserve the wholesome, farm-kid image. At times, it felt more like a conservative religious group than a youth leadership organization. To enjoy the great parts about it (and there were many), I had to put up a false version of me, like an alien putting on her "human suit" to go out among the masses.

Once I got to college, it just got worse. Despite my declarations to my family, I had the sinking feeling that they were right: people like us *didn't* go to college. I knew I deserved to be there—that I had more than earned my place in academic terms—but I still didn't feel a sense of belonging. While everyone else had time to hang out with friends, I worked thirty-plus hours a week off-campus to pay for rent and food. While other freshmen opted for a traditional dorm experience, I couldn't afford that option, so I rented a house with some guys I knew through the FFA. And while my roommates were kind and safe (in the sense that I didn't have to deadbolt my bedroom door at night), I still didn't feel like it was okay to be all of me.

I'd come home from waitressing all night to find my roommates and their girlfriends hanging out on the couches. I'd get a lukewarm, "Hello," and a few side-eyes, but otherwise at times I felt it was best to stay out of their way. A trusted friend filled me in on just how much my roommates' girlfriends had to say about me when I wasn't there, "Can you believe Amber works at Hooters? *So unprofessional* for someone who was a state FFA officer. I'd *never* let my daughter work somewhere like that."

Yes, I worked at Hooters. No, it's not a topless club (apparently, this is a popular misconception). It's just a restaurant where servers wear tank tops and tiny shorts. And honestly, the biggest reason for working there—other than needing to pay rent and buy food—was that I didn't feel judged there. My fellow Hooters girls became some of my best friends, even to this day. In one way or another, we were all hot messes at the time, so we weren't about to judge each other's shortcomings. Was there drama and gossip? Sure. Were there ugly moments? Definitely. But, interestingly, it was far less anxiety-provoking than slinking past the good-ole-boy roommates and their mightier-than-thou girlfriends at the end of a long shift.

(As a side note, I'm still connected with some of those roommates. And while it was hard back then for us to respect each other's different life choices, we've learned since then. Three cheers for personal growth!)

I had a false belief that I could only be worthy and respectable if I wore grandma shoes and didn't show my shoulders. That I was a "slut" because I was on birth control. That I was somehow tarnished because I had a job my friends' parents wouldn't approve of. And yet, simultaneously, I knew that I *liked* these things about myself— my style, my work ethic, the way I took responsibility for my choices, and my willingness to do what it took to improve my life.

This—the contrast—is why truth and authenticity can be so fucking hard.

To fully unleash your truth, you have to be willing to *become* that ideal you're searching for.

Sometimes, your truth doesn't match any identity that you've experienced before, or even anything you've seen from others or on TV.

Sometimes, you have to be willing to do what others won't. Like transforming every friendship in your life. Like moving on from your college roommates to share a house with a forty-five-year-old male stranger, because at least there you can breathe. Like learning how to be truly alone when all you desire is to be loved and recognized by the world—because learning to love yourself is more important than being validated by others.

People like us will do all of that—and so much more—to be who we truly are.

Your rules may be different from those you've grown up with or accepted. Recognizing this is the first step to freedom. And so, you have a choice. You can get okay with the side-eyes, the uncertainty, and the moving on. Or, you can keep trying to zip your beautiful, sparkling self into a small, drab, "good girl" uniform that no longer fits. It's up to you.

Before you say, "But, Amber, it's too hard!" and go looking for the nearest rock to hide under, let me remind you: *You don't owe them anything.*

You don't owe them the hiding of pieces of yourself.

You don't owe them the fitting into their world.

You don't owe them a version of you who looks, and sounds, and thinks exactly like them.

You don't owe them your time, your money, your tears, your love. You most certainly don't owe them your one and only beautiful life.

You don't owe them anything.

You don't need to fit in with the jocks, the geeks, the farmers, or the rockers. And yet, you can hang with all of them, and enjoy the heck out of every moment. Because when we fully accept ourselves, there is no other acceptance or love that's truly necessary. We stop looking for validation from other people, and just let them be who *they* are, too.

THE TROLLS WILL ALWAYS BE THERE

Once, when I was in my early twenties, I was hanging out with my extended family. Someone brought up a hot topic, and I assertively shared my point of view.

My aunt rolled her eyes, and said, snippily, "You're just like your father."

I knew right away what she meant. And it shut me down.

My father. A funny, larger-than-life guy. A my-joke-must-be-heard-by-everyone-in-the-room kind of guy. A guy who's too big, too loud, too brash (by hoity-toity standards, anyway). A guy who also was, at times, demanding and aggressive, and who, after a long day of work, required every female in the household to be at his beck and call.

You're just like your father. It stung, as it was meant to. And it came with so much confusion.

Confusion, because I had opinions. I had jokes to tell, just like my dad. Did telling them mean I was trying to dominate the room? Was having energy and an interesting point of view the same as cutting others off or speaking over them? I didn't believe that having something to say was the same as demanding that all eyes stay on me.

But loved ones around me were painting me with that brush.

More, they were instilling into me their false belief that an empowered woman is a demanding bitch, and that a young woman who can hold a room is "aggressive."

People will shame you for a whole fuck-ton of things. However, in this journey, I've come to understand that *they can't shame you if you don't allow it.*

For years, this was one of those "easier said than done" things. I didn't know how to shut down the shame—until I did.

In 2011, three years after forming my first band (and about a year into our first original band), we did what every rock band was doing in 2011: we made a recording and put it on MySpace. However, what the "rule book" on how to be a rock band failed to mention was that people online can be real assholes.

I put our song up on our page—and then, a few days later, excitedly logged in to see if there were any comments. Did our fans love the recording as much as we did? Did other bands want to book us to open for them? It felt like opening a giant doorway of possibility.

Then, I started reading the comments.

"Your singer sucks! She can't sing!"

"Get a guy singer."

"You might be okay if you got rid of the chick."

I was sobbing by the end, but I still had to laugh out loud. Here were these trolls telling my bandmates (aka, my husband and brother) to get rid of me, when it was my damn band!

I decided then and there that the band would continue, even in our apparently infinite suckery, for as long as I felt like singing, because *I started the damn thing.*

I can hear you saying, "See, Amber, that's why I'm not putting myself out there! That's why I'm not speaking on stage, starting a business, wearing whatever the heck I want, trying that new punk haircut ... because look what happens! You get *decimated.*"

I'd agree with you, except ... it's not true.

Yes, the trolls were out in force. But I wasn't decimated—well, not after those first awful minutes, anyway.

Nope, that shitty experience was an opportunity for me to look at myself and make two powerful commitments. First, to never let anyone steal my joy. And second, to ask, "How can I get better?"

Some of the comments referred to my singing as "pitchy." And guess what? I *was* pitchy. So what? Was I going to stop doing something that brought me joy because of what some faceless douchebag had to say about it on MySpace? No way.

When I look back on my life, I want to see what a badass I was. I want to see a woman who lived her joy. Not a woman who went into hiding because someone didn't like her singing.

"THERE IS NO RULE THAT SAYS THEIR HATE GETS TO BE MORE POWERFUL THAN YOUR JOY."

So if you want to head for the hills or scream at the top of your lungs whenever you think about going all in on who you are, just remember: the only rules you have to live by are the ones *you* create.

There is no rule that says you have to listen to the trolls—even if one of them is your snarky aunt, or your partner, or your best friend. Even if one of them is the voice in your head.

There is no rule that says you have to accept criticism.

There is no rule that says some random dude's opinion gets to have value in your life.

There is no rule that says their hate gets to be more powerful than your joy.

THE BIGGEST, MOST BONKERS BELIEFS

So, how do we take the first step (or the hundredth) toward unleashing our truest selves? More, how do we do it when we aren't even sure which parts of us belong to us, and which have descended upon us from our parents, our lineage, and those who influenced and guided us?

The first step is *feeling*.

Unadulterated feeling. That juicy, terrifying, "If I'm being completely honest with myself ..." feeling. A big part of our work in this book will be learning to tap into that—how to peel back the lies from the raw skin of truth.

It all starts with being willing to ask the big questions.

While I was researching for this book, I posed a question

to my online community: "Have there been times when you've knowingly held back the fullest expression of yourself, despite a desire to live into that expression? If so, why?"

The answers I got astounded me.

The first several answers were from other women in rock and metal bands. They responded quickly, with comments like:

"I struggle with negative self-talk."

"I worry that I'll look stupid if I try something new."

"I convince myself that I don't matter, and that no one cares. That I don't deserve to be successful."

Woah. Here were my badass rock-goddess sisters—some of the fiercest and most authentic women in my world, whom I admire and look up to—opening their death-metal hearts to me in a comment thread.

It didn't stop there. Looking back at my groups over the last several months, I noticed that even the most confident-appearing women are often plagued by self-doubt beneath the surface. What this indicated to me was that, if even the boldest of the bold—the bravest of the brave—are still to some degree holding themselves back, surely the same is true for the rest of us.

I sat with tears streaming down my face as the moment of clarity came. Even when we appear free, we may not be free. Even when we are outwardly rocking it, we may still feel ugly, unwanted, and unworthy of love. Even when we appear to be Unleashed, we may still be tied down and terrified to move.

And we *accept* this. We think this is how it has to be.

You're reading this book because you believe—you *know*—that you're a badass goddess who is ready for something more than the façade. You are ready to own your rebel self, face your fears, and say a giant "Hell, yes!" to your free-spirited genius. You are ready to shape that half-belief, those "maybe" moments, and your secret dreams into your whole, shining, everyday truth. Because that truth is *who you are.*

The more I play in this space of unapologetic badassery, the more I realize that the things I felt "bad" about for most of my young life were exactly the things that made me ... well, me! And the beliefs that made these things "bad" or "wrong"? They were complete and utter bullshit.

I felt bad for wanting clothes that were nicer than the hand-me-downs that I received for years—*and* my truest self is highly expressive with her appearance.

I felt bad for being too boisterous when it made my introverted sister shrink into the shadows—*and* my truest self owns whatever room she's in, simply because her energy is big.

I felt bad for asking too much from my parents—*and* my truest self knows how to receive from others and the Universe like the badass goddess she is.

I felt bad that my cousins all went on vacation together and my family did not—*and* my truest self loves a good adventure.

I felt bad for wanting to sit at the adults' table and being told to go away—*and* my truest self is a natural leader who claims her seat among other powerhouses.

I felt bad for spoiling my parents' efforts at playing Santa Claus because I did not fall for those tricks—*and* my truest self is highly intuitive and perceptive.

I felt bad for having hopes, dreams, and goals that extended well beyond the walls I grew up in—*and* my truest self knows she is limitless.

I felt bad when others didn't like me or thought I was weird—*and* my truest self knows that my willingness to embrace myself just as I am is a superpower.

Do you see how this works? On the other side of the "feeling bad" is a huge truth about who you came here to become—a soul awareness. If it wasn't part of you, and important to you, you wouldn't feel bad about it when you experienced the opposite. You'd be happy in conformity.

I know this duality so damn well. I've been a performer for nearly my entire life, in one way or another—and I've been singing professionally in bands since 2008. It took nearly ten years for me to get to a point where I could flip that "feeling bad" to connect with my gifts—and, as a result, connect with my audience without worrying what people were thinking. What's interesting is that, at the same point when I flipped those fears, my band Morningstar started taking off in a meaningful way—with people staying after shows to meet us, give us hugs, ask us to sign posters, and tell us about how our music has impacted them.

When we're too busy feeling bad—or trying to control the bad feelings by manipulating how we are perceived—we lose the magnetism of authenticity. We lose the essence of our unbridled spirit, our shine. And, most of all, we lose our ability to create real connection.

When you get out of your head and flip the "feeling bad" into being *you*, you will form the deepest, most pure connections with other humans.

When you know who you are—when you see yourself, and finally allow yourself to be seen, regardless of what others think or feel, you have arrived on the threshold of your full self-expression.

That's when you are Unleashed.

FLIP IT, BABY!

When you make the flip into soul awareness—from "feeling bad" to owning your truest self— you will start to access some really juicy information. You may discover some parts of your life where you've been inching toward full self-expression, and you're closer than you thought. You may discover other areas where you're not only still in the box, but you've tried to nail the lid shut. From the inside.

Sometimes, coming to terms with the things you want is a process in and of itself. Sometimes, this looks like wanting to uncouple or have a nontraditional relationship. Sometimes it looks like a dream to leave it all behind and spend the rest of your life on a beach in Bali. Sometimes it looks like revealing a big secret—like your authentic sexual orientation, or your desire to completely abandon your "respectable" career.

But most of the time, flipping from "feeling bad" to soul awareness is more subtle. It starts with a tickle that soon becomes a gnawing. Or, it's a heaviness, like you're carrying your body weight in rocks. You know that you're feeling bad about things, but you can't quite put your finger on why. Life starts to feel like a grind.

When this happens, remember: You always have a choice. You can be who you came here to be. You can claim your birthright to be authentically you, and share that as a gift with the world. You can choose joy over judgment. You can give the trolls the middle finger.

Or, you can keep feeling bad. It's up to you.

Take my friend Peggy, for example, whose strong-headed, "lone wolf" attitude was really a response to "feeling bad" about asking for help. It took her getting strep throat three times in three months before she could finally admit that she needed help in her life and business.

The great thing about knowing someone for twenty-plus years is that you have access to all of their backstory. Peggy grew up on her family's dairy farm, and we met in high school through the good ol' FFA. She excelled in all areas throughout high school and college, and after graduation went straight into a leadership position in a notable company. Later, she became a mother, the editor of a major publication, and an entrepreneur. With so many balls in the air, every day felt like a juggling act. But Peggy was convinced that to "do life right" she needed to do life on her own.

Over the years, I've seen her muscle through all kinds of situations. She is one of the most capable people I know. And, when she finally got her voice back after that third round of strep throat, she was finally ready to see it too.

"Why do I feel like I have to do it all, all the time?" she shared with me. "When did that become a rule in my life?"

When we're living our lives by a standard that we didn't choose to create, it's important to recognize that it came from somewhere. But where? I had some ideas, but Peggy ultimately came to her own conclusions (because she's strong-headed and self-sufficient like that), and this is about *her* truth, not mine.

As we talked, it started to come out. Her hard-working mother was a strong-willed, determined woman who stood firm in her faith and convictions (and wasn't afraid to share her opinions about either). She herself had grown up being forced to be independent early and, after birthing three kids, had also taken on the role as head farmer, head of household and a care-giving role for her husband. Peggy's mom was the farm director and the dedicated mom, the person who did whatever it took to keep everyone fed, clothed, and running on time. She had zero time for feelings, emotions, or drama. There was no one to count on but her. She was strong, and she did it all.

In Peggy's own efforts to do it all, she was unknowingly modeling her mother—a woman who led through command and grit, without meaningful support, because she had no other choice.

As a child, Peggy felt bad that her mom had to do so much alone, so she learned to do everything for herself, and to be a bit stern with herself. But, on the flip side, her soul awareness wanted her to be soft, not hard—to receive as well as give, and to experience real connection instead of an endless stream of to-dos. She desired to be fully present with her children. To soften into connection with like-minded women. To unpack and reframe her life to make space for joy, not just work.

The question then became: by embracing what her soul awareness was showing her, who would be left "feeling bad"? Her mother? Society?

Peggy realized that her old Rules for Living were, in fact, a direct response to "feeling bad"—a list of ways to mitigate the shame and self-blame of situations that were challenging for her, or to please people who meant the world to her, like her mom. Her new Rules, however, were all about soul awareness. And she couldn't live by both at the same time.

Once you commit to stepping into your soul awareness, you'll begin to rewrite those rules in perfect alignment with the life, and the *you*, you want to create. We're going to play a lot in this space throughout the rest of this book.

But for now, you gorgeous, badass goddess, remember ...

Only *you* write the rules you live by.

And you don't owe them anything.

CHAPTER 3

OUR PERSONAL TRUTH IS THE PATH TO FREEDOM

When 90 percent of the people you call think you're a scammer and hang up on you, but you still make sales, you learn that you can sell *anything*.

Starting my senior year in college and three years afterward, I worked as a contract salesperson—aka, a telemarketer. I cold-called people who were traveling to trade shows and sold them hotel accommodations over the phone. While it sounded sketchy to many people at first, it was a legitimate business, and I used my "fit in with anyone anywhere" abilities and good ol' Midwestern work ethic to bridge the gap and make sales.

Then, a friend referred me to a new digital marketing position within a TV station advertising sales department. Ever wonder how commercials get put onto TV programs? Salespeople go out and find advertisers! At first, I was hesitant because I didn't know if I was cut out for working for others in a "normal work environment." I had been selling hotel rooms from a basement, over the phone, while pacing around like the Wolf of Wall Street for the last four years. I didn't even know what a "normal job" with a salary and benefits was. But I figured that selling digital marketing, or ad slots, or whatever it was, couldn't be nearly as grueling as telemarketing!

The hiring process was a bit weird—like, when I was navigating conflicting information between the local manager and the higher-ups with whom I'd interviewed—but I was too excited to see the red flags.

I had a rocky start. Between colleagues who saw me as

a competitor (when I was actually a collaborator), dueling managers, and people who simply weren't willing to have their industry disrupted by a twenty-six-year-old with long, fiery violet hair and the digital age, there were a lot of highs and lows. I'm sure that my lack of ascribing to "corporate culture" didn't help things either. I cried multiple times a week—at home, in my car, even at my desk—all the while logging fifty-five-hour weeks. But while I longed to fit in and be accepted, my experiences in college had taught me not to make that a goal. Instead, I focused on becoming the best salesperson I could be ... and I crushed it.

During my five years with that company, I broke records and repeatedly landed on the company wide Top Ten Salespeople lists. I was successful. I was, after that first awful year, celebrated. More, I finally had money for things—like a mattress that came from the store and not from the trash. (Yes, I was so broke when I got my first apartment that I had to junk-pick a mattress.)

And yet, I felt disconnected. Until I'd been at the job nearly a year, no one on my team even knew that I was a hardcore weekend rocker. I turned down my style, my hair, and my volume to seem "professional"—aka, acceptable to those around me. In so many ways, it felt like I was back in that stuffy FFA uniform, pretending to fit in when in fact I was longing to just be the true me.

You know that feeling—that squeeze, where you can't fully catch your breath? When the weight of all of your unfulfilled dreams starts to crush the life right out of your soul? That's where I was. And the pressure kept mounting.

I was running out of time to make a real go with my band, and playing regular gigs wasn't very manageable with my 8:00–5:00 work schedule. Going on an actual tour was certainly out of the question.

I wanted to escape. I wanted to blow shit up and run for the hills. But I didn't feel like I could—because that million-pound brick on my chest was made of gold. One hundred and forty thousand dollars a year, to be precise. That's the amount I was on pace to earn that last year in my role, more than double the commissions I'd earned when I started five years earlier. I was achieving at levels I had never imagined. I *liked* my new lifestyle and the possibilities that came with it. How could I drop it all and start over?

It's so funny, the tricks we play on ourselves. One would think that, given the skills I'd accumulated and the prestige of my sales record, it would have been easy to walk away. But, perversely, the struggle it had taken to rise to my current success was my biggest reason not to move on. *I fought like crazy to get here*, I told myself. *It has to be worth it if I worked so hard for it!*

What I didn't realize was that there is no starting over. Whatever we learn, we take with us. It becomes part of us—another layer of our being.

Hoping that a shift in mindset would alleviate some of my struggles, I started reading more blogs and inspirational quotes. Things like, "Chase your passion, not money!" and "Trust that when you find your path the money will come" stood out to me. If this was true for others, could it also be true for me?

"WHATEVER WE LEARN, WE TAKE WITH US. IT BECOMES PART OF US— ANOTHER LAYER OF OUR BEING."

Nope, I decided. It could *not* be true for me. After all, the people who'd authored these quotes had come from more money than me. They had backup. They had support. They probably had it easier growing up. They were all from California, not the Midwest. They were not like me. I was a special case, and I had special challenges.

This thought process held me back for months. There's a difference between being special and unique—as all of us are—and thinking we're some sort of renegade species to whom the universal human rules of possibility, mindset, and growth don't apply. No matter what is standing in our way, we have a choice about how to be with it, and how to shift it enough that we can move forward.

In the end, the only thing responsible for the crushing weight on my chest was my own fear. My potential wasn't tied to my company, or my current clients. My past wasn't a limiting factor for what I could create for my future. If anything, the fact that I did rise to such levels of success was an indicator of what I could create again or anew, for my future. I recognized that if I wasn't achieving my potential, it was nobody's fault but mine. And if I ignored the voice that had started whispering within me—the same voice that had whispered about becoming valedictorian and going to college—it was my own soul I'd be disappointing.

By pretending that I was a special unicorn to whom the rules of growth and success could not apply, I was giving my power away. And, as the months rolled past, I began to realize that that was no longer acceptable to me. The whisper had become a shout, saying, *There's more for you!*

THE WHISPER IS REAL

As I shared in Chapter 1, Africa has always been part of my consciousness. I never knew how, or why—it just was. In college, I had the chance to do a study-abroad program in Kenya for close to a year, which was an unforgettable experience. (I'll share more about that in Chapter 4.)

In 2015, ten years after my college exchange program, my husband and I booked a trip to Kenya for my best friend's wedding. It would be the longest vacation we'd ever taken together (two whole weeks!) and we'd need to leave our beloved doggies behind.

Just before the trip, something started to shift within me. It was as if my soul was taking the reins. As they say, the heart knows before the head does.

I started dreaming about what I would do if I went out on my own as an entrepreneur—what I would offer, and who I would work with. I even began a conversation with a copywriter to plan what my (still imaginary) website would say. Looking back, I find it strange that I took those actions without actually having decided to leave my sales job—but I also know now that living in flow looks like that sometimes. It was almost like an out-of-body experience.

Fast-forward several weeks and we're on this magical trip in Kenya. My husband Brandon and I spent a few days alone at a tent camp in the Maasai Mara. During that time, we got to slow down for a moment to appreciate how far we had come in our individual journeys since we'd first met seven years prior, and in the life we'd built together. We talked about my budding idea to build my own business, and of course, he was fully on board.

We spent several days after that traveling around with my friend's family and the rest of the wedding party in a *matatu* (basically a big van) and catching up on life. It was then that I announced that I was going to leave my job and start my own company.

I expressed my views on how there could be a different way of doing business. Something different than the corporate world I was immersed in. I shared the need I saw in my local market, the problems that my future clients were having, and how I planned to create the solutions. I shared my desire to serve from a place of care and love. To create a workplace where people's strengths and uniqueness would be celebrated, and how different I would feel because of it. I would get to choose how I showed up every day and who would surround me in that journey, and shape a company culture that was fully aligned with my vision and values.

I let my heart speak. And all the while, that $140,000 brick on my chest felt heavier and heavier, until I felt like I was suffocating.

Could I really do this? It had to be an all-or-nothing thing, because what I wanted to build would have been considered a conflict of interest with my current job, so as much as I wished I could start that business as a side gig at first, I couldn't.

I wondered: How long would it take to find enough clients to replace my income? Would I ever replace my income?

Why had I worked so hard throughout my twenties to build my current sales funnel, sacrificing happiness, fun, vacations, nights out with friends, if I was going to just *walk away?*

And yet, there I was, riding in a van across the Kenyan wilderness, telling my best friend's whole family that I was going to burn it all down to "follow my purpose." Because that whisper I'd been hearing was my soul, and the fear of not discovering who I was meant to become was bigger and scarier than all of the unknowns.

Maybe hitting the "six figure" mark isn't a big deal to you. It isn't for many people. But for me—given the constant struggles with money with which I was familiar—it was huge. It was more money than anyone in my family had ever seen, and it meant that I finally had options that I longed for my entire life—like not having to worry constantly about how to pay next week's rent, or how to fund the next emergency car repair.

But in the end, it didn't change what I was feeling on the inside. In fact, the more committed to that money I got, the heavier the brick became. That pile of money was literally grinding me into the ground.

What I didn't realize then was that life is built on a foundation of *being*, not achieving. I had been busy setting goals, winning accolades, and making money, but the harder I pushed, the less of my true self I was *being*. By staying fully engaged in a sales job that required me to do the same thing day in and out, without room for much innovation, I was not in inner alignment. Could I have made great money and be set for life? Sure. But I wouldn't have been comfortable with selling myself short. In my sales role, I wasn't leading with my intuitive and empathic gifts to their fullest; in fact, most days, they made me feel like a crazy, emotional train wreck.

To actually unleash who I was meant to become, I had to let the perceived "guarantee" of money—and the security that came with it—go.

When the voice said, "Let go of the money. You've survived on much less before, and you can do it again," I listened. Because I could no longer *not* listen. Speaking about my desire to change the landscape of business had triggered a huge unfolding inside of me. I was now on a mission—and that mission was far, far bigger and more important than $140,000 a year.

I had no idea how we would pay our bills. I had no idea how much our lifestyle would change. But I chose to believe my heart, not my head, and my heart said, *"I believe in you."*

You know that whisper, too. The fact that you're reading this right now means you've heard it, and you're willing to give it an opportunity to grow louder in your life. You might not yet even know what that soul-voice is saying—and that's okay. You are on your path toward an Unleashed life, and you will hear what you need to hear in exactly the perfect time.

Everyone's situation is different. We all face fears, unknowns, and challenges. Maybe you need to let go of the money thing—or maybe you need a damn budget. Maybe you need to slow down, or maybe you need to speed up. And yes, we are all special—but none of us are a renegade species to whom the universal rules of possibility, mindset, and growth don't apply.

So, listen. Believe.

And, when possible, make a plan.

WHAT'S YOUR BRICK?

If you've heard the whisper of your soul, but you're still holding back, chances are you have a brick on your chest, too.

You feel it when you turn inward. You feel it in the effort to breathe, to relax, to just *be* for a moment instead of doing more, more, more. You feel it when you think about something bigger, brighter, or just different in your life.

That brick, my friend, is made of false beliefs.

I had a false belief that I was only worthy of making money if I worked really, really hard.

I had a false belief that money that came easily and without strain wasn't "earned," but taken.

I had a false belief that I wasn't knowledgeable enough to run my own company.

I had a false belief that people wouldn't take a young female seriously in the sales industry. That they wouldn't take *me* seriously, because I didn't conform.

And somewhere, deep down, I still held that false belief that "people like us" didn't do the kinds of things I was dreaming about—that I was, and always would be, an imposter.

All these false beliefs told me I wasn't ready to tackle what I'd envisioned. But, they were all wrong.

That's the thing about a soul whisper. It doesn't come when you *feel* ready. It comes when you *are* ready. When you hear it, you don't need to wait until next year, or next month, or even tomorrow. You are ready because you heard the voice of your soul—and your soul is waiting.

If you're truly craving an Unleashed life, your job isn't to vet or verify what your soul whisper is saying. It's to find out where you are censoring yourself, limiting yourself, or holding yourself back—and then bust through those blocks so you can take the action you're being called toward.

I'm not saying you have to do what I did and quit your job on the spot. There's a discovery phase, and an action phase; you cannot have transformation without both. And often, it's through the discovery that we uncover the actual thing that is ready to transform—whether that's an external factor or, more often, something within ourselves. When you accept that you will never *feel* ready, you realize that you are actually further along than you imagined.

Leaning into your soul whisper is the preliminary step in the Unleashing Process—the same process I use with my private clients to create lasting freedom, true self-expression, purpose, mission—and, of course, money flow.

If you want to live an Unleashed life, you will need to do three things:

Uncover your dreams and decode those soul whispers you've been hearing.

Unlock your potential and build the confidence to remove your "bricks" and fully believe in yourself.

Unleash your impact into the world by taking action to create the amazing life you desire, including rich purpose and profitability.

So far in this book, we've been working through the "Uncovering" phase. You've awakened to your whisper and begun to see where your false beliefs about yourself and the world have been holding you back from the awesome, inspiring, authentic life you crave and deserve.

Your personal truth is the path to freedom. Whatever your soul is saying, it's time to listen. You are who you are for a reason—even if that reason isn't clear yet. As we work together over the course of this book, you will learn how to trust this, embody it, and eventually live it out loud.

These days, I know that I'm in true alignment when I unapologetically bring my heavy-metal, Saturday-night stage self to the boardroom. That same sexy, creative, give-it-all-you've-got energy is flowing through my mind and body whether I'm helping a client create authentic connections with their consumers or singing my heart out with my band on stage. I might be flexing a different set of muscles, but I'm still the same person—*Thee* Amber, the one I was always meant to become.

I won't pretend that it's always easy or comfortable to bring it all, all the time. Authenticity isn't a one-and-done event. It's a beautiful, messy, awkward exploration that

"AUTHENTICITY ISN'T A ONE-AND-DONE EVENT. IT'S A BEAUTIFUL, MESSY, AWKWARD EXPLORATION THAT UNFOLDS ACROSS A LIFETIME."

unfolds across a lifetime. But even in those moments when I'm scared to death, I can still breathe.

I want that for you, too.

So, right now, out loud, I want you to declare your intentions. Whatever's been on your mind to create, whatever version of yourself you're being called to become, say it now. Out loud. Own it. Give those vocal cords over to your soul, and see what amazingness comes out of your mouth. If you've got a microphone laying around, plug it in and belt it, baby.

Don't turn this page until you've fully declared yourself. Because from here on out, we're going in deep.

Your soul knows you're ready. Do you trust it?

Four, three, two ...

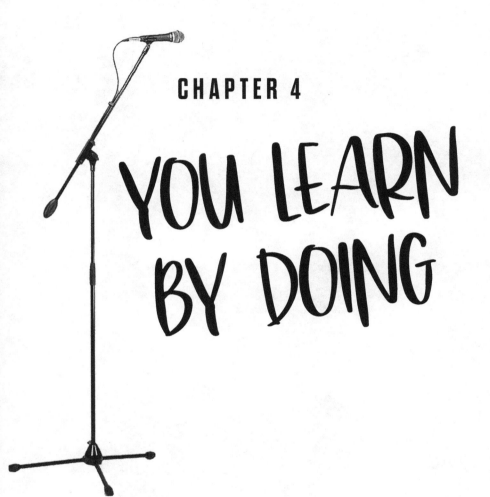

CHAPTER 4

YOU LEARN BY DOING

Not many people my age remember reading newspapers, let alone finding their spouse in one.

I would never have anticipated meeting my life partner that way, either—but hey, when it feels right, you need to go for it. Even when it seems crazy.

Before I tell you that part of the story, let me backtrack a bit.

As I've mentioned, Africa had been with me for as long as I could remember; it was like a silent undertone in my young life, a place that felt like a magical connection. When, during my freshman year, I learned that my university offered a study-abroad program in Kenya, I immediately started learning Swahili and preparing for my junior year abroad.

I wasn't clear on much at that point in my life. But I did know—even if it was in a vague sort of way—that I wanted to be connected to a global world, explore cultures beyond my own, and positively impact humanity in some way. I also knew that I wanted to become Miss America and have a rock band.

So, my plan was: study abroad in Kenya, become more "worldly," come home, win pageants, and live out my dreams of rock stardom. While all of this was happening, I'd finish my undergrad degree in International Relations, work in an embassy, and you know, change the world and stuff.

Go ahead and laugh. We've all learned to poo-poo our idealism and our big, audacious dreams. We're told we aren't "realistic." But if we don't start with our dreams—however far-out and naïve they might seem—and follow the thread from there, we will never come close to living Unleashed.

My study-abroad program was supposed to be four months, as I couldn't afford the tuition for the full year. However, once I got there and experienced the freedom of being in a new environment—and actually got some sleep, since I didn't have to run multiple bartending and waitressing gigs between classes—I decided to extend my stay to a full year. I wanted to explore Kenya, and also explore more about myself. That exploration required taking out yet another school loan to cover my expenses, but I figured I had the rest of my life to pay for it, so why not?

I came to Kenya as a bright-eyed, well-intentioned yet quite ignorant American who was going to "help save kids in Africa." I departed a more humbled, grateful, and informed person. I also came home about twenty pounds heavier from all the lard cooking and chapati bread—but this, too, I learned to be grateful for. In a part of the world where many people were hungry, having access to plenty of food was something to appreciate. As my host mama Rosie always said, "Ahh, it is very good to be fat!"

At the end of that year, my eyes and heart had been opened wide, but my life plan hadn't changed a whole lot.

Step 1: Return to the US, graduate college, become Miss America (more on that last one later).

Step 2: Work at an embassy, thereby getting exposed to new cultures, somehow improve the world.

Step 3: Form a badass rock band.

It was Step 3 that stopped me in my tracks. While music exists across the globe, I just couldn't connect the dots around how I would create a femme-metal rock band and find gigs in the bush of Djibouti or the desert plains of Turkmenistan.

Plus, my school debt was racking up fast, and it was stressing me out. I couldn't add another year at university to "figure it out." So, I changed my major to Political Science, which would still allow me to graduate within four years, and flew back to my small hometown to spend what was left of the summer living with a girlfriend and bartending in a small town near to where I grew up, before returning to college for my senior year.

I was totally unprepared for the reverse culture shock. I had gone from one extreme to the other twice in twelve months—in terms of environment, yes, but more so within myself. I was peeling back the layers of who I was—what I truly believed about myself, not just what my programming told me.

And, of course, at the same time, trying to figure out how to become Miss America *and* a rock superstar ... while saving puppies along the way.

Heading into my senior year of college, I had started my first sales job. I spent my days in school, rushing home to my dingy efficiency apartment between classes to squeak out cold-call sessions. Smile and dial! While it was a tough job, I soon started seeing the payout from it. I started making $200 a week in commissions, then $500 to $1,000 a week ... a few times I even earned close to $2,000 a week in commissions, all while finishing my college degree. This newfound way to make money felt like a path to freedom; it was almost addicting.

I had been waitressing for years by this point, so I understood the concept of "hustle harder, make more." Take more tables, take the extra shifts, work overnights on New Year's Eve when everyone else wants to party. Be kind, quick, humble, and funny. It was intense, but way better than earning minimum wage at a checkout counter like some of my friends.

But this sales thing ... this was a whole new level of money. I learned to weave my gift for human connection with strategy. Have a conversation, ask good questions, bring solutions. I learned it wasn't about what I needed (which was to sell), but rather about the problem the customer wanted to solve.

I didn't realize it then, but this "Wolf of Wall Street" sales job was laying the foundation for what would later become a thriving career as a brand and business strategist. I had found a piece of the "core-truth" me, as well as a valuable skill set. But the rest of me? It was falling by the wayside as I hustled and ground and chipped away at what felt like a mountain of school debt.

After graduation, I moved away from the big city where my college dreams had come true, and found myself returning to my rural roots, where I had a boyfriend "back home," with no real direction except that I wanted to "make some money" and continue working my remote smile-and-dial sales job.

For a while, I forgot the plan.

By March of 2008, the relationship I'd been pursuing

had fizzled, and although I had a decent job, my goal to "make money" wasn't my only motivation any longer. The real me felt like she was wilting away on the inside. For a while, I couldn't figure out why—but then, I remembered the whole reason I was back in Wisconsin and not off in the desert somewhere working for an embassy. *The rock band!*

I started researching "how to start a rock band" and scrolling through listings on Craigslist and Backpage. (Yes, back then that was a legitimate tool for musicians!) Then, one day, a friend called me.

"Am, I found it! An ad seeking a singer for a rock band!"

If you're unfamiliar with the ways of small-town newspapers, let me clue you in. They cover the whole spectrum of local news, from the latest high school sport team performances to the annual county fair or festival—but the biggest section is the classified ads. Right there, smack dab between the rummage sale listings and free farm cats, was my future.

"Wanted: Singer for a rock band." I immediately picked up the phone.

A few days later, I got a call back. The guy on the other end seemed a bit shy, and excused himself several times to hiss, "Shut up!" at whoever was making noise in the background. I was slightly confused, as I assumed that my bandmates would be young like me; this guy sounded like he had a house full of unruly kids. I was a bit more concerned that he was telling them to shut up. But something told me to trust.

"

BEING UNLEASHED IN YOUR LIFE REQUIRES ONLY TWO THINGS: TRUST AND ABOMINABLE PERSEVERANCE.

"

A few emails and awkward phone calls later, we chose a date in April to meet up for an audition. The guy explained that he, his brother, and a friend were starting a band and needed a singer. He also explained that they lived in the middle of nowhere with no phone reception, so it would be easiest for him to meet me at a local gas station so I could follow him out to the property. (If I hadn't been raised in a rural area where these awkward situations are typical, I might've thought twice about following a guy in the dark to a remote environment without phone reception.)

It was a chilly April evening when I pulled up to the aforementioned gas station. The snow and ice were still thawing, and I was shivering because I'd worn a cute top and jeans, and everyone knows rock stars refuse winter gear at all costs.

My potential bandmates pulled up in a hot, midnight-blue Pontiac Firebird. The guy in the driver's seat rolled down the window, peered at me from under his mop bangs, and, flashing the most adorable dimples you ever did see, said, "Hi! You can follow me to the farm."

I grinned at his childlike excitement ... and simultaneously noticed that this guy didn't look a day over eighteen.

I followed him to the farm and, in a few chaotic minutes, found out that it hadn't been his kids I'd heard in the background, but his four younger siblings.

We jammed at top volume in his family's freezing cold garage as the farm cats milled around, and a band was born.

I didn't know it then, but I had just taken a few more steps toward the center stage of my life.

You see the guy driving the hot blue Pontiac was Brandon, my now-partner in music and life. He was eighteen-turning-nineteen to my twenty-four, and, as he later told me, he experienced a sense of fate that night, too. "I figured I'd better play it safe, so I brought my good car out of storage, and wore my best Hollister shirt. You know, just in case you were hot. And you were."

From Kenya to a Northern Wisconsin gas station, I had followed a thread. It didn't always make sense—but I was learning to trust it.

We were kids with a dream, crappy equipment, and a cold, drafty garage to rehearse in. But we were also possessed of a willingness to suck before we got better. We chose to see beyond circumstances and hold ourselves accountable to our goals. When, in the early years, people told us we sucked, or told Brandon they should kick me out and get a new singer, we kept going, and supported each other to strive for more.

We got pushback in other areas, too. At one point, one of my dearest friends said with concern, "Brandon seems very nice, but ... you're a world-traveled college graduate, and he's hardly left home or experienced life."

I completely understood their perspective. I knew exactly how our relationship looked to the outside world. But I also knew the truth of how it was on the inside, between us. I wasn't looking for someone to "complete" me. I was looking for a relationship to invest in. I wasn't playing around, and I wanted a partner who was all-in on supporting my goals, just as I would support his, so we could build something together. Otherwise, we'd be wasting our time.

Starting out, we definitely struggled. While I had stayed in my cold-calling sales job out of college, sales had gotten a lot harder during the recession. Plus, I had a lot of new bills pouring in (like student loan payments, a car loan, and health insurance, for starters). Brandon was still in tech school and struggling to find a minimum wage job. By the time we were ready to rent our first apartment, we were saddled with debt and strapped for cash.

Long story short, I was ecstatic when I found our first piece of furniture—a mattress—in the trash. We were grinning like crazy while we hauled that thing up to our apartment. Once it was on the floor (since we didn't have a bed frame), I launched into a fully-stretched "freedom jump" with arms and legs spread.

"We have a bed!" I whooped. "No more sleeping on the floor!"

Mortified, Brandon hauled me off of it, shrieking, "Let me at least spray it with Lysol!"

ABOMINABLE PERSEVERANCE

Being Unleashed in your life requires only two things: Trust and abominable perseverance.

In your journey to living a more truth-aligned and authentic life, you're going to have to make decisions and do things that are *way* outside your comfort zone—most often, long before you think you're ready. You're going to have moments when you feel uncomfortable. Small. Less than. In fact, you *need* to live those moments to stand a chance of living Unleashed.

Why? Because learning requires doing. You can't do better if you never do the thing in the first place.

If you *do* it, you get to see who you are *in* it. You get to taste it. And you get to change, course-correct, and improve so you can have a different experience next time.

We can't change other people or *make them* value us. But we can change how we see and value ourselves. We can trust that where our hearts call us are precisely the places we need to go—and we can keep going, even when the road gets rough.

Living Unleashed looks different for each of us. But *everyone* who lives this way has made friends with perseverance. They've learned to stand in the outcome, even when it hurts. They've learned how to fall flat on their face and get back up.

Today, when I struggle with self-doubt—when I question whether I'm doing enough, or being all of me—I pause, and take a moment to reflect on how far I've come.

From the trash mattress and Lysol to a beautiful home of our own.

From the abject mortification of having to put back a box of noodles at Walmart because I couldn't afford them, to buying healthy organic food options.

From the time we canceled a long-awaited trip to visit my best friend because our car broke down and we couldn't afford to repair it, to becoming "snowbirds" and wintering in tropical locations.

From that time someone said I sucked at singing, so I deleted our song and cried for days, to being a role model to other women rockers.

From that time my aunt said I was "just like my father," and I felt ashamed for my vivaciousness, to speaking on national stages about true authenticity.

When I pause long enough to clearly see how far I've come over the course of my lifetime, I find the strength to go on.

We all have struggles. And while it may appear that many of my struggles were rooted in money, what they were really rooted in was *identity*. I'd be willing to bet that many of yours are, too.

What does it *mean* to be someone who is *worthy* of a new mattress, of a pay raise, of confidently owning the stage like the rock goddess (or stud) that you truly are? What does it mean to be someone who is *Unleashed*—who defies convention, expectation, and norms, regardless of the judgments thrown their way?

It doesn't matter whether your biggest struggle was how to pay for food, or arguing with your parents about which college you'd be attending on their dime. It doesn't matter if your struggle was against a person or an institution. We all need to fight, in some way, to blossom into our true selves and unleash our full power. It's just that, for some of us, that true self might be buried deeper, and the layers of trauma and conditioning might cling tighter.

Regardless, one thing is true: you've come a long way, baby. You didn't get here by hemming and hawing and "feeling ready." You *learned by doing*—and because you did, you took another step closer to your true self.

You know what that makes you?

A *badass*.

THE RAD BADASS LIST

Do you actually *remember* all the things you've overcome? If you did, would it change your perspective?

This simple yet powerful exercise, which I call the RAD Badass List, has helped my clients make important decisions to do stuff like: speak up for themselves to earn partner status at a law firm; confidently increase their service rates; totally revamp their business model; pursue their first speaking gig; and more. Whatever you feel a calling toward, you have the capacity to do!

The Badass List reminds you that you can do scary stuff, because you are RAD!

RAD stands for Reflect, Acknowledge, Do it again! It's a simple process you can use anytime you need a reminder of how far you've come, and how powerful you are.

Here's how to do it.

"WE ALL NEED TO FIGHT, IN SOME WAY, TO BLOSSOM INTO OUR TRUE SELVES AND UNLEASH OUR FULL POWER."

STEP 1

Make Your Badass List. This is where you REFLECT on your biggest wins. Write down the biggest, most important things you have accomplished in your life. All the hard things you overcame. All the times you were just ... a badass. What did those things change within you? What did you learn? Consider key times when you had a goal or a dream—something you were striving for but weren't sure you could accomplish. Think about how you almost gave up, but pulled through with flying colors. (Yes, you totally have those times! Don't be shy. Get them down on that paper!)

STEP 2

ACKNOWLEDGE how you felt in the struggle and in the win. Choose one of your biggest badass moments from the list you just made and reflect on how you felt *right before* you achieved it. What were you feeling and saying to yourself in the months/weeks/moments leading up to that victory? For example: maybe, in the last few weeks leading up to completing your degree, you were running on fumes. You were working, raising a family, and trying to study for finals all at once. What did you tell yourself that got you through? When you started your business but hadn't yet secured your first client, how did you keep going? Or, that time you were asked last-minute to speak to a room full of people, and were so afraid with your stomach in knots that you almost backed out, what made you say, "I'll do it?" Once you've acknowledged your "before" feeling, think about how you felt when it was over—when you stepped across the stage to get your degree, or got that first contract, or got the standing ovation. Feel *that* feeling.

STEP 3

DO IT AGAIN. You've struggled. You've been afraid. But you still achieved your goal and grew through a challenging situation. This is irrefutable proof that *you can do it again.* The next time you are struggling with a decision or moving through a scary change, revisit this list to remind you that you are already a badass. Feel it. Own it. And then, claim it!

Anytime that you feel doubt, revisit your Badass List ... because you are RAD!

MANUFACTURING CONFIDENCE

Discomfort leads to results—*if* you're willing to do something with the discomfort beyond just moping and feeling like shit.

You already know that you learn by doing. When you follow the thread of your desire, trust it, and persevere, amazing stuff will happen.

But did you know that the doing also creates confidence?

So many people think that confidence is innate—that you either have it, or you don't. But confidence is not a have or have-not; confidence is *manufactured in the process of taking action.*

In the beginning, when you're stepping in a new direction or trying something new, you're testing an unproven hypothesis. So, instead of letting it feel big and scary and final, treat it as an experiment! You can "try on" this new version of you by creating an alter-ego who is a match for this new way of being in the world. After all, the only way to know if the boots fit is to try them on! So, maybe you're channeling Wonder Woman, Gloria Steinem, Superman, or Beyonce. Or maybe you make up a character (like Fierce Fiona or Sophisticated Sam) who you can embody like an actor on a stage. If it's not the everyday "you" who's taking a big, brave step forward, the process can feel a bit less overwhelming.

Now, I'm not personally an advocate for using an alter-ego as an ongoing practice. It can work in the short term as a confidence-booster, but in the long term it can actually undermine your growth, because you never come to a point where you stop hiding and protecting the "real" you—your ego—from the potential for hurt and disappointment. In fact, the most impactful and lifelong transformations happen when we become so free from ego that we can't help but be our true selves in every situation.

So, if it helps, use an alter-ego to "act as if" while your ego learns to trust your truest self. Test out different ways of being and see which actually resonate in practice. Stand up when you want to sit down. Speak more boldly. Sing more loudly. Get more visible. Give yourself a chance to play in different energies to see how they feel—and, above all, do what it takes to manufacture the confidence you need so your true self can shine.

"Learn by doing" is the final piece of the Uncovering phase, where you are coming to awareness about your true self, desires, priorities, and values. In the next chapter, we'll be leaving the Uncovering phase behind and stepping into the Unlocking phase, where you'll start living your new awarenesses and prioritizing your values, alignment, and joy. However, the "learn by doing" phase will never truly be behind you. Every time you enter a growth curve, you have an opportunity to become a next-level version of you who's even more awesome, even more authentic, and an even bigger badass.

PART II

UNLOCK

CHAPTER 5

THE SEVEN-INCH PLATFORMS

When I was seven, I decided I wanted to be Miss America.

I would watch the pageant every year on TV. I even made my own score cards and notes. I dreamed of being there under the lights, wowing everyone with my utter awesomeness and proving that even "people like us" could do big, important things.

But the real draw for me, even as a kid, was the confidence and poise of the contestants. How intelligent and brave they seemed as they shared their hopes, dreams, and opinions on live TV in front of an entire country. How the contestants considered their stances on politics and social issues. I wanted a slice of that.

In high school, I wasn't able to compete (as I wouldn't get far without money, support, or training) so my strategy instead was to first focus on building my credentials. College, volunteering, and studying abroad in Kenya ticked a lot of boxes.

I entered my first pageant during my senior year of college. I had two years left before I "aged out" of the Miss America program, and I was determined to make them count.

Over the next two years, I competed in about seven or eight pageants. Each one taught me something new about how to navigate the pageant world. But they also revealed two glaring issues.

One was my boobs. They didn't fit properly into any dress or interview suit, and cute swimsuits were totally out of the question.

This challenge wasn't new to me; I'd been trying to work with my breasts for years. Granny bras, double-layered tank tops, and excessive slouching were all tactics I had mastered by this point. In fact, I was so used to hiding my chest that it was hard to stand up straight onstage.

In the end, I dished out the money for a custom-made dress and interview suit tailored to provide the extra space my body needed without looking like I was wearing a parachute.

What sewing and costumery couldn't solve, however, was my second problem: a lack of pageant-appropriate talent.

At that time, talent accounted for 35 percent of a contestant's score. The private interview was 25 percent, evening wear 20 percent, lifestyle and fitness (aka, swimwear) 15 percent, and the onstage question a mere 5 percent.

Damn. My best skill was talking.

Where other contestants had grown up with years of dance, piano lessons, and vocal training, I'd grown up singing along to cassette tapes of Alanis Morissette, Nirvana, Joan Jett, and Pat Benatar on a microphone plugged into a cheap stereo. It was a far cry from classical training. I didn't know how to read music. I sang from my soul, which felt awesome and powerful, but there was no telling what might come out.

A pageant coach once suggested I sing "Orange Colored Sky" in an orange dress, and in a moment of misalignment, I agreed. I have freckles, a golden skin tone, and the wrong voice for that song. The next option was dancing and singing to "All That Jazz"—but I'm not a dancer. I took a few quick adult dance lessons, tried my hardest, and even performed it twice, but ... let's just say it was less than inspiring.

And so, at my final pageant, I decided to do what set my soul on fire. I would sing a soul-belting, gritty-rock version of Pat Benatar's "Heartbreaker."

Hell yeah, baby. Pat had always been there for me. Now I was here for her—even if neither of us fit the pageant rule book. I would rock for both our sakes.

And rock the pageant world, I did.

Earlier, when I'd chosen "pageant-appropriate" songs, my best placement had been first runner up—close, but not a winner. I'd received great feedback from the judges: *Highest interview score I've ever given. Amazing stage presence. Needs to work on a stronger talent.* All of this to say that I was great in some areas, but I still wasn't ticking all of their boxes.

After that first-runner-up placement, I didn't give up on pageants, but I did give up on "All That Jazz." That meant going all-in and baring my rock-n-roll soul. I figured if I couldn't win by their rules, why not play by my own?

And so, for my very last pageant appearance, I stepped on stage in seven-inch platform heels and lacy leather pants, and belted "Heartbreaker" like my soul depended on it.

In some ways, I guess it did.

I didn't win that pageant. I didn't even place. But I stepped back more fully into my rebel spirit—even though it was uncomfortable. Even if it left an entire auditorium of people speechless.

I can only imagine what that room full of pageant moms, directors, and hopefuls were thinking as I belted, "Your love is like a tidal waaa-ave ..." in my gritty-rock voice. It makes for great giggles.

When I chose "Heartbreaker," I gained the confidence I needed to stop bending, molding, or shape-shifting to conform to rules that were out of alignment for me. I put it all out there. I lost the chance at a title, but I gained something much, much more precious: the kind of confidence I'd dreamed about when I was just a kid with a homemade scorecard.

If I can't win while being me, it's not a win at all. Ever.

PUT ON YOUR CROWN AND SASH

I still give props to anyone who participates in the Miss America pageant. It's a wonderful program. It just wasn't for me. When I realized this, I was able to stop feeling rejected and start choosing myself—even if being *Thee* Amber didn't come with a crown and title.

It's exhausting playing by others' rules to get ahead. But "just go be your true self" isn't exactly helpful advice, either—even once you've gone through the Uncovering process and have actually decided what "being your true self" looks like.

Choosing our path of truth comes with risk and sacrifice—but it also lets us choose which risks, and which sacrifices, are actually worth it.

As ambitious people, especially women, we choose against ourselves all the time. The titles, the positions, the relationships—even when they get us ahead, they can come at a cost. Every time you compromise your true self or shrink to fit the box, it chips away at your soul. More, it prevents you from taking steps toward what you truly desire.

So, let me ask you: what if honoring yourself is a far greater win than any title, promotion, relationship, or accolade?

I'm not implying that you have to trade in your power suit for leather pants. (Unless you want to—and in that case, rock on!) I'm just asking that you pay attention to the small things. Like saying yes when you mean no. Like wearing black when hot pink is really your color. Like saying yes to a bar crawl when you're really craving a night at home with Netflix and Ben & Jerry's (and want to wake up feeling good the next morning). Like hoping your partner will treat you better, instead of finding someone who actually will.

Yes, sometimes you have to make temporary concessions to get to where you really want to go. You might need to stay in that boring job to provide security for your family while you build a runway for your future business. (Or, maybe you simply choose to keep the job and find fulfillment for your passions outside of work. Nothing wrong with that either!) You might need to keep the peace with a family member during your brother's wedding even though you really want to scream. You might need to make slow progress one step at a time, instead of blowing up your whole life in pursuit of the change you desire.

But in most cases, the cost of conformity is just too high— and it's your job to discern when it's costing you too much. If you want to live Unleashed, it's time to put your true desires

"CHOOSING OUR PATH OF TRUTH COMES WITH RISK AND SACRIFICE— BUT IT ALSO LETS US CHOOSE WHICH RISKS, AND WHICH SACRIFICES, ARE ACTUALLY WORTH IT."

first and release the rest. Obligation energy is in no one's highest interest. Not even the people you're capitulating to.

One thing I hear a lot from clients is, "How can I tell when I'm actually honoring my true self, and when I'm not?"

This is a big problem for many people. Each of us is a complicated blend of our true selves, our personalities, and our conditioning. And sometimes, when you bend so much, and sell yourself short so often, you might forget that you're even doing it. Maybe you've bought into the narrative that suffocating on the inside is just normal, and that it's your job to stay small and safe.

Sometimes, it's the tiny cuts, not the big storms, that shred our sails.

And so, when you're ready to take the stage as your most raw, real, and authentic self, it's not going to be all Care Bears and rainbows. You may have to do some scary-ass shit, like:

- Trusting your instincts and speaking up at a team meeting instead of waiting to be called on.
- Signing up for your first public speaking gig.
- Explaining to your mother that you love her dearly but need your space.
- Leaving everything behind to get out of an abusive situation.
- Quitting a job or switching jobs before you feel ready.
- Investing in yourself and your business, even if it means changing your lifestyle or taking on temporary debt.

Those are scary decisions. They aren't right for everyone. But they might be right for you—and they may be right, *right now*.

In order to make decisions like these from a place of empowered alignment, you need to know two things: *who you are* beneath the conditioning, and *what you value.* This is how you will know if you are actually honoring your true self, or just taking on another set of "shoulds." More, you have to be willing to put who you are and what you value on full display, like your crown and sash, so others can know you by them.

Are you ready for that?

YOUR GUIDING PRINCIPLES

You've already learned a lot about who you truly are through the Uncovering processes we've explored together in this book. Now, we'll lean into your guiding principles and values.

Guiding principles are the beliefs that come from within you that steer your decisions. They inform how your life is lived and how your work is done, often without you even being aware of them. They're not the same as other beliefs, in that they're not limiting or constricting; instead, they feel right, all the way down to your deepest knowing.

Becoming aware of your guiding principles is powerful because it allows you to make more aligned and informed choices and lead from a soul-centered place, while at the same time releasing feelings of shame, guilt, and people-pleasing.

You don't need to feel bad about saying no to something that directly conflicts with your values!

Here are a few examples of the guiding principles that steer my work and leadership within the Soul Seed brand and onstage with Morningstar:

- Your truth is the path to personal freedom
- Progress over perfection
- Stay judgment free, Embrace curiosity
- Resistance is opportunity
- Trust your intuition
- Soul informs strategy

These guiding principles give me and my team a unified set of beliefs to steer the work. See how they serve as a steering compass?

To discover your own guiding principles, answer the following questions:

- What are the statements or favorite quotes you often find yourself saying about how business should be done?
- What are statements, philosophies, or favorite quotes that you believe people should live by?
- What are your anti-statements, the things you'd *never* be okay with as behaviors in life or business?

Review these answers and reflect on what stands out about the deep inner beliefs that shape your life.

YOUR VALUES

In addition to guiding principles, it's useful to define your core values, which are energies informed by your guiding principles, and which in turn inform your actions, like this:

Guiding principles >> core values >> actions

A lot of people think of values as statements like "teamwork," "honesty," or "integrity." But without a definition for what those words mean *to you*, and how they look in practice, they aren't very useful.

For example, my top personal values are Authenticity and Personal Freedom. Some people might interpret those in the context of "civil liberties," but that's not at all how I think about them. To me, Personal Freedom means the freedom to be exactly who you are, and stand in your truth, in any given moment. Every decision I make either supports me to live in that value, or it doesn't.

So, when zeroing in on your values, think about the ideal behaviors you want to exhibit in work and life, and work backwards from there. Soon you'll be guided to further clarify the behaviors you desire of yourself and others that you work with. This process helps you to live in greater alignment in all areas of life.

Here's a short exercise to help you identify and understand your core values:

- Step 1: Draft the ideal behaviors that you'd like to see in yourself. For example, you might say, "I desire to stand in my truth no matter what the situation."

- Step 2: Draft the ideal behaviors you'd like to see in people around you. What draws you to someone? What instantly turns you off?

- Step 3: When you look at your answers from Steps 1 and 2, what words or phrases sum up the ideals you've identified? Make a list of statement words that feel aligned.

- Step 4: Write a list of what would *never* be okay for you or others to do in each of the following contexts: relationships, career, and business. These are your "anti-values," which tell you what you will not compromise on.

- Step 5: What are the opposite values to your "anti-values" from Step 4? For example, if "lying to a client" would never be okay for you, write down "Honesty" as the opposite value.

- Step 6: Reflect on what this exercise revealed about your top core values and your personal truths, and how this knowing will change your decision-making processes from this point forward.

- Step 7 (Optional): An additional step, which is particularly useful for business owners and in team settings, is to create an Excel document which lists your values one by one in their own columns across the top row. Just below each value, draft a definition for that value in the context of your business. Next, in the furthest left-hand column, create rows for: Superior, Above Expectation, At Expectation, and Below Expectation. In these rows you will draft a behavioral description for what it looks like to apply this value at a superior level, an above-expected level, an expected level, and a below-expected level. In a business context, this helps everyone on the team to understand what your values look like in practice so that they know what it actually means to demonstrate teamwork, accountability, integrity, etc.

Two of my favorite marketing phrases are, "The more you narrow your message the wider it goes," and, "You can't be all things to everyone, but you can be everything to someone." The gist is, the more you focus your message and niche on serving your most aligned and ideal customer, the more successful you will be.

The same applies in your personal life. The more you allow yourself to live in alignment with your guiding principles and use your values as your steering compass, the easier all your decisions become—and the more joyful life becomes, as you won't waste time and energy on priorities, places or people that aren't truly a match for you. Whenever you question a decision or feel off-track, pause, and ask yourself: "Is this values-aligned for me?" Listen closely enough, and you will always get an answer.

TRUTH IS GREATER THAN FEAR

As freeing as it was to step onto the pageant stage as *Thee Amber*, I was kind of sad that I didn't win. My rebel spirit was satisfied and proud—but the small, scared part of me that was still working to be "accepted by others" felt hurt and raw. I wanted to be me—but I still wanted to be liked by everyone. I wanted to belong in the box and out of it, all at the same time.

On your journey to honoring your truth and living in alignment with your values, there will be moments that make you rethink your decisions to speak and live as all of you. No matter how badass you are (and you *know* you are), there will be part of you that wants nothing more than to turn around and erase yesterday's decisions.

This happens to everyone.

Old wounds and trauma can get triggered. Conditioning can grow claws when it wants to keep hold. Imposter syndrome can make you wonder if you're just a big bullshitter pretending to be a badass.

Your inner knowing and connection to your authenticity doesn't free you from fear, but it will keep you on your path to freedom. Personal freedom is something only you can create, and that absolutely nobody can take away from you.

These days, I proudly own the title of Pageant Reject. I love the guts and gusto of that younger version of me—and I've racked up a lot of ridiculous stories that my friends can tell at my Celebration of Life party someday. More than that, I have a truly epic item to add to my badass list. I survived the eye-daggers and open-mouthed shock of those pageant moms and prim judges; not much else in the world of "visibility" can hold a candle to that.

Trust me, no one will ever tell the story of how you shrink-wrapped yourself to suit their expectations, or how much it touched them that you sacrificed your authenticity on the altar of their demands. What they'll remember is how you challenged them, made them see things differently, and lit up their lives like a bonfire.

So, let me ask you: what do you want your friends to say at *your* funeral?

WHAT ARE YOU SACRIFICING TO "WIN"?

Where in your life are you still going against your own internal grain in order to win? In order to please others? In order to play by the rules? In order to fit in? What piece of your authentic truth is being silenced so you can play by the pageant rules?

Some things are not worth sacrificing to "win."

Which things *are* worth sacrificing is for you to decide.

This discovery process starts with a question: "What goals in your life require you to be a different version of you to succeed?" Once you know the answer, you can decide if that goal is still in alignment with your truth,

"TRUST ME, NO ONE WILL EVER TELL THE STORY OF HOW YOU SHRINK-WRAPPED YOURSELF TO SUIT THEIR EXPECTATIONS, OR HOW MUCH IT TOUCHED THEM THAT YOU SACRIFICED YOUR AUTHENTICITY ON THE ALTAR OF THEIR DEMANDS."

your guiding principles, and your core values. Is what you *think* you want *actually* what you truly desire?

It's possible that what you seek requires a different and more aligned version of you. A version of you who can fully receive it, allow it, and become it. A version of you who's not afraid to be themselves. A version of you who says no and means it. A version of you who shines like a star and doesn't apologize for it.

Other "opportunities" require a version of you who sits down, shuts up, and plays nice. A version of you who hides who they are when they're at the office, keeps their true desires secret, or feels like they have to "tone it down" to be part of the club.

The former is an opportunity to lean in further, peel back any fears that are keeping you stuck, and allow the best you to come through. This is the space we are playing from together.

The latter starts with what's happening "out there," and applies those conditions to you—which is exactly what you are working to break free from.

Sometimes, when you take on a new role or step into a new thing, you will feel momentarily accepted. We think, "I played by the rules, and it worked!" But, over time, you start to feel like a half-formed version of you once again. You feel split. This is beyond compartmentalizing. It's segmentation.

If you desire to live in authenticity and alignment, it's useful to learn to recognize where you are gaining false fulfillment by fitting someone else's rules. Your guiding principles and values will be your best barometer for this.

My coach and friend Darla (who I'll tell you more about in Chapter 9) describes this dynamic as the difference between a "Big-T Truth" and a "small-t truth." A small-t truth is a limiting belief that you hold about yourself or the world, but which doesn't align with who you authentically are and who you desire to become. When you recognize the small-t truths you're holding onto, you can begin the process of shifting that energy and uncovering your Big-T Truth—the truth you know deep in your soul, the one that's calling you forward to live Unleashed.

When I made the decision to be all of me, all the time, in all places in my life, it "cost" me my corporate job and several connections and friendships I'd made over the years. It wasn't easy. But, as I shared, striking out on my own was the clear next step in my authentic journey. Staying where I was would have required me to be a different, smaller version of me. To "win" my freedom and claim my truth as a leader and visionary, I was willing to sacrifice who I was and the perceived security I had created as that version of me.

Maybe, as you're reading this, you're starting to recognize some patterns in your own life. Maybe some truths are coming to the surface about how you've been playing by others' rulebooks. Maybe those truths are about small things: the way you show up with a particular friend, or the things you do and don't tell your parents during your Sunday phone calls. Or maybe your truths are bigger: a partnership or marriage that is truly not aligned, an unclaimed gender identity or sexual orientation, a totally new model for work and career.

In my work with clients, we sometimes find that big things are wanting to shift, heal, and realign. Sometimes, you just have to blow shit up and start over. More often, though, it's the small things that are really preventing them from stepping into their fullest self-expression, impact, joy, and fulfillment. When they recognize those tiny moments of resistance—the daily feeling of grind, the tightness in their chest, the way they catch their breath when they're holding back what they really want to say—they can create massive shifts without all the pyrotechnics.

OPPORTUNITY VS. OPENING

No matter who you are, where you come from, or what field you work in, you're going to get a lot of opportunities in your lifetime.

I'm casting a wide net for the definition of "opportunity" here. It could be any of the following: a job offer, a new relationship, a role in a play, singing in the church choir, playing with a band, a mastermind or peer mentorship group, volunteering with a community organization, a new leadership role, or any new or different activity or way of expressing yourself.

At first, when opportunities come, they look cool and shiny. But not every opportunity is a doorway to a more aligned and authentic expression of you. So, you'll want to evaluate whether the opportunities coming your way are openings to something greater—openings that will support you to become more expansive, more expressive, and more grounded in your truth—or just another place where you will need to put on the hand-me-downs, hold back, or censor yourself.

First, consider the opportunity (job, friendship, relationship, expression, etc.). When you look at what it represents—to you and in the world—can you get behind it? Do you truly feel good about it? Or is there something about it that goes against the grain of your being?

Second, what is the cost of doing this (or not doing it)? When you get honest about it, is the cost something you can live with, and even get excited about? Or is the cost going to be some aspect of your truth, values, and authenticity?

I can't even tell you how many times I've watched people keep themselves stuck by saying, "The opportunity was too good to pass up," while explaining away a violation to their soul. Sounds harsh, right? Well, the truth can feel harsh when it bumps up against our conditioning.

When something feels "off" and goes against who we are in our core, but we proceed and do the thing anyway—stay in the relationship, take the job, hire the person who's qualified on paper but doesn't gel with our team—isn't that a direct violation of self?

The next time you get that feeling in your gut, like something just isn't sitting right, don't explain it away. Don't look for excuses to do the thing anyway. Never agree to sing "Orange Colored Sky" in an orange dress unless that's *really* your jam, just because the pageant coach tells you it will fly. Instead, ask yourself what you truly want to do,

"PROGRESS DOESN'T NEED TO MEAN BLOWING IT ALL UP. IT JUST MEANS DOING A LITTLE BIT MORE THAN WE DID YESTERDAY."

and what you truly believe. Then, see if it lines up with the opportunity that's presenting itself.

I'll be honest, that feeling of rubbing up against my truth came up several times in the writing of this book. I had an opportunity—writing a book—that I could approach in one of two ways. I could write exactly what was in my heart and soul, and share my truth. Or, I could talk circles around what I really believed so I wouldn't hurt or offend anyone.

It wasn't easy, but I chose my Big-T Truth. I chose the version of me that I'm being when I feel most aligned, most authentic, most empowered, and free of fear that's driven by ego. I chose *that* Truth, because you and I both deserve better than a half-hearted rendition of "All That Jazz."

I'm not asking you to be "perfect" in this new expression of authenticity. I'm just asking you to choose alignment more often than you choose holding back. Progress doesn't need to mean blowing it all up. It just means doing a little bit more than we did yesterday.

SPACE FOR SOUL

Does your life ever feel like one big run-on sentence?

We're always busy. Always on to the next big thing—the next book, the next project, the next thrill. Sure, this is fun—but when it comes to things like identifying aligned opportunities, space—not speed—is key.

The work I've introduced in this chapter will require you to take a breath. Step back. Find a new perspective. While making your RAD Badass List and evaluating your opportunities through the lens of your truth may not seem like time-consuming activities, you still need breathing room to evaluate what you know about your truth and authentic self. You need space to consider who you want to be, so you can decide what is most aligned for you right now, and for where you see yourself going. If you're serious about creating truth and freedom in your life, you can no longer allow yourself to get caught up in what's already been done and all of your current responsibilities and that degree you have that should really get used and the commitments you made that no longer feel aligned and what your friends will think if you change your mind ...

Pause. Breathe. Give yourself some space.

Space doesn't necessarily just equal time. When I joined the pageant scene, I was in college with a full course load, in over my head with classes I didn't feel equipped for, working thirty hours a week to pay rent, and fitting pageant stuff in in my spare time. There wasn't a lot of space in my schedule to lean into alignment. Where I did have lots of space was in my environment, emotionally, and energetically. I was a world away from my childhood home and all of the personalities and opinions there. I had freedom to move in my new town, and thousands of new people around me—people with different beliefs, ideas, and backgrounds from me. That space helped me to explore, try things on, and discover who I wanted to be.

Since then, I've created space in many ways—by leaving my corporate job, by taking vacations (and staycations), by changing up my inner circle, and by never saying no to an aligned opportunity to be onstage. It's been a case of progress over perfection, but each time I find myself up against the wall, I know I'll also find a stick of dynamite to blow my way free—if I'm brave enough to use it.

So please, make space to identify and neutralize your small-t truths so you can step into your Big-T Truth. That space might come as time, or it may be energetic or emotional space away from the things, places, and people that are depleting you. Make space to test out this new view of life and authenticity. Make space to explore your freedom. Make space to consider whether your opportunities are also openings to something more. Make space for your Big-T Truth. Make space to step out onto your own stage, put on your crown, and own it.

And, when in doubt, put on some Pat Benatar, sing your heart out, and ride the tidal *waaa-ave*.

CHAPTER 6

BOUNDARIES

As a kid, I asked Santa Claus to make my parents get divorced.

Growing up, I witnessed and took on all sorts of emotional traumas from my household. I couldn't understand why people who loved each other fought so much, and why they kept themselves in what, at times, felt like misery.

We are each a product of our personalities, upbringing, societal conditioning, and genetics. I was raised with good ol' Midwestern family values. Work hard. Don't ask for too much. Stay humble.

In our household this also meant, "Deal with it. Suck it up. Stuff it down. Shut up and work. Drink if necessary. Resign yourself to doing things you hate. Stop your whining and get it done because there's cleaning to do and bills to pay."

Due to this mentality, my parents' communication was often off-track. Playing by the rules of "deal with it," they often struggled to say what they were actually feeling, and so said ... just about everything else. That caused challenging conversations to spiral into arguments. No matter how well I played my role as family counselor, we just couldn't get it together.

I attributed a lot of anxiety to finances, even though I knew money wasn't the root of the issue. I constantly encouraged my mom to charge more for her cleaning services. I even researched the going rates for house cleaners and found they were *three times* what my mom was charging. However, when I pleaded with her to raise her rates, she replied, "If people think I'm worth it, they'll give me a raise on their own."

Needless to say, hardly anyone ever did.

By the time I left for college, my painful wishing that my family would actually *deal* with their deeply rooted traumas had morphed into frustration and anger. I was in a place known as the "trauma aftermath"—the period between when trauma happens and when healing begins. *These people,* I thought, *have stayed in a vortex of hurt and dysfunction, and they've taken me along for the ride.* During college, I spent as little time at home as I could, not because I didn't love or miss my parents, but because I was angry, hurt, and needed space away from everyone else's "stuff" to figure out who I was and who I wanted to be.

Years later, once I began to come to terms with my childhood and heal the things that weren't mine to carry, I realized that I'd learned many great things growing up in my family. "People like us" may not have gone to college (until I came along), but we knew a lot about acceptance, generosity, and staying humble. Either of my parents would give a complete stranger the shirt off their back— even if they hardly had a shirt to give.

All gifts—including the guiding principles and core values you uncovered in Chapter 5—have a shadow side. The shadow side of "giving the shirt off your back," is that you can deplete yourself. You give to the point where it becomes toxic—and then, you get pissed off, because people are taking everything you give and asking for more. But you never change anything. You just let it brew and brood and fester.

At least, that's how it worked in my family, because as much as we knew about generosity, one thing we didn't know about was *boundaries.*

And that, it turns out, was the root of just about everything that hurt us as a family.

Boundaries, particularly when it came to boundaries that put my family's well-being first, were definitely not for "people like us." Boundaries were something my mother "felt bad" for having. Years of generational and emotional trauma had taught her that she wasn't worthy of making her own empowered choices, or of saying "no." Besides, how could she possibly put herself first and help others at the same time?

More, there was simply no space for either of my parents to explore or comprehend how they felt about the bigger issues in life, or how greatly their own traumatic childhoods had impacted them. They had just enough time and energy to put meals on the table every day—a luxury they hadn't always had as children.

So, when I started finding and defining my own boundaries as a young woman—first around my education, then around my pageant experience, my band, then in love and business—it caused more than a little friction with my family, my friends, and our small-town society. I loved my parents and they loved me; there was never any doubt about that. But there were a lot of intense highs and lows every time I talked to them, and even more when I spent any face-to-face time with them. I saw how they were on different wavelengths about what they actually wanted, but couldn't communicate those wants in a clear way so that the other could support them. I saw how they'd aim to be kind to others and give, give, give while completely bypassing their own hurts. (This is a pattern I saw later in myself, and that I still see with many clients. We tell ourselves that if we're good people and help others, that should be enough—and serving others does feels good! However, no amount of giving to others will magically heal your own internal hurt if you refuse to address it.)

As a child, I had learned to live in a place of perceived responsibility, trapped between defending my parents and making excuses for their shortcomings, while also feeling intense anger and frustration at them for not taking responsibility for their own healing. When I did spend time with them, I took on the role of family counselor. I took it *all* on.

When I started to bring my newfound knowledge of boundaries into our relationship in my late twenties, it was hard to walk the line between being a daughter who is there for her parents and being an adult who refuses to take that shit onto her own shoulders. I still struggle with that dynamic—but I meet it head-on, because I know that's the only way to ensure that my family trauma ends with me.

That is my responsibility.

REPEATING THE PATTERN

By the time I started my band, got married, and launched my business, I was feeling pretty good about where I was in life. I had put distance between myself and my past, and was doing things differently.

Or so I thought.

You see, when you aren't experienced with boundaries, those old patterns and paradigms tend to rear their heads in the sneakiest ways. Like the time just over a year into my business when my dad and brother came to visit from out of town.

Spending meaningful time with my dad wasn't something that I had a lot of memories of. He worked a lot while I was growing up, and we didn't share a lot of the same interests. When he unexpectedly retired early due to an injury, he suddenly had a lot more time on his hands—so, when he asked if he and my brother could come for a mid-week visit, just because, I said yes. This was new territory, and I was excited to see how this turn of events might strengthen our relationship!

At that point, I was also dealing with some serious stress in my new business. Having followed through on my commitment to create my own work path, I was now "doing it all"—bringing in clients, serving existing clients, managing daily business tasks, and even getting ready to hire my first employee. I felt like I was teetering on a precipice, getting ready to take yet another big, scary step into the unknown.

Until my dad came to visit, I hadn't taken so much as an afternoon off since I started the business. Now, I was stepping away for *two whole days*, including an afternoon trip to visit some relatives we hadn't seen in a long time.

As we were driving to our relatives' house, my phone rang. I glanced at the screen, and my heart skipped a beat. It was Carrie, a client I'd been working with for the last few months. She'd hired me for brand strategy and web design, and despite the dozens of extra hours I'd spent on the process, she still wasn't pleased with what we'd accomplished.

I'd been trying for weeks to get her on the phone so we could talk through the edits she wanted, instead of trying to do it all by email. (We'd already discovered that lots of things can get lost in translation!) Now, she was finally returning my call—right as I was stepping away for a few precious hours with my family. I felt totally overwhelmed. What was the right thing to do?

I let the call go to voicemail. Three long minutes later, the message alert dinged.

"She left me a three-minute voicemail? This can't be good," I muttered.

My dad, not usually one for comforting words, did his best to offer up an alternative possibility. "Maybe it's nothing? Don't get worked up when you don't even know what she has to say."

Good advice. And, on this occasion, wishful thinking.

My dad and brother could tell I was a ball of anguish and stress. So, we pulled over, and my dad took the wheel while I climbed into the backseat to listen to the voicemail and do whatever it took to diffuse the situation.

I pressed "play" and put the phone to my ear.

Hi Amber, I hate making this call, but I need to get this off my chest. This website isn't anything like what I wanted. There are so many things wrong with it. It's not at all what I had in mind, and since you're the expert, I shouldn't have to be the one to tell you how to make it better. I convinced my husband that we needed this website, and now I look bad.

He's saying it was a mistake and I'm regretting my decision. I hate that I have to tell you these things, but this whole situation is just really unprofessional, and I expected more. Call me back. Thank you.

My heart sunk lower than low.

At this point, we had already redesigned the site two times, going well beyond the scope of work outlined in our contract. I wasn't upset that she was disappointed with the design; I knew by now not to take differences in opinion personally. Rather, I was filled with fear and frustration that a client whom I'd already gone over and above to serve had so little respect for me and my work. We had already redesigned the site a second time without charging, and now she had changed her mind about what she wanted, which was fine, except she was blaming us as if we had made a mistake. She wasn't valuing my efforts, even though what she was asking for was *way* beyond the scope of our agreement.

I felt small.

I felt mixed up.

I felt self-conscious.

I felt pissed off that I couldn't make her value me.

And, at the same time, I felt bad that I'd let her down when I just wanted to make her happy. I was terrified of what she might say to our mutual friends. I was ready to do whatever it took to salvage the situation, even if it cost me time, money, and my sanity.

Wanting to do the "professional" thing (because how dare she accuse me of being unprofessional when she'd just left a voicemail like that!), I quickly emailed Carrie to say that I received her message and would call her the

"ONCE YOU'VE HAD YOUR BOUNDARIES VIOLATED ENOUGH TIMES, YOU START TO SEE THAT THE COST IS ALWAYS HIGHER THAN YOU ANTICIPATE."

next day. Then, I did my best to suck it up and come back to the moment—a moment I was supposed to be enjoying with my family.

Honestly, the only thing I remember about that afternoon was how awful and distracted I felt. I was there, but not there. I was locked in my racing mind, doing my best to find a solution that didn't leave me feeling gross, undervalued, and just plain furious.

It took several days before I was able to calm down enough to see the situation clearly. But when I did ... ooh, boy. It was a zinger.

You see, I'd let Carrie violate my boundaries. When she overstepped and asked for us to redesign the site a second time (despite us having designed it according to the mockup that she had previously approved), I didn't push back. In an effort to "give," and help her out, I just did the work she asked for, while internally getting frustrated and shifting the blame to her. "She's so *rude* and *demanding*!" I fumed. But the truth was, I had never set an expectation that showed her how I wanted to be treated. I simply let her walk all over me. How could I rightfully be pissed at her when she wasn't shown the boundary?

Had I spoken up about the project going out of scope, reminded her that she had in fact approved the mockup from which the website was built from, and given her clear options for next steps, Carrie would have been able to make an informed decision about how she wanted to continue. Of course, her response might have been the same—demanding that I just fix it—but perhaps I wouldn't have felt taken advantage of, and I would have been better equipped to hold my ground toward a fair solution rooted in clear agreement terms.

At the time, it seemed like reiterating the terms of the contract, holding Carrie to our agreements, and speaking up would be emotionally and energetically draining for me. Far easier to just do the work, I reasoned. You know, "Suck it up, stuff it down, be a good person, and do for others."

But once you've had your boundaries violated enough times, you start to see that the cost is always higher than you anticipate.

And then, I realized something. I was letting Carrie violate my boundaries in the same way that my parents allowed everyone to violate theirs, including how they violated each other's. There was no difference. I was in this position because I had refused to take a stand for myself, and had made other people's comfort—in this case, Carrie's—more important than my own. I let her dictate to me the worth of my time, energy, and work.

Holy shit was that a hard one to swallow.

As a sensitive person who cares about integrity (and, let's face it, my reputation), it was gut-wrenching to finally tell Carrie that I had fulfilled the contract as stated and any further work would be billable. But afterwards? I felt freer than I had since I started my business. I was no longer waiting for my client's approval; instead, I took a stand for the worth of my work.

People will treat you exactly as you allow them to. And most of the time, they won't have any idea why that's a problem. Why? Because the only way for them to know whether they've crossed a line is for *you to tell them where the line is*, and what the consequences of crossing it will be.

I began to understand why, in earlier times in my business, it had been hard for me to increase my rates. Even after all my growth and healing, some part of me still believed that other people could dictate my worth, and the worth of my work. I had been shown that I was only worthy of money if it was hard-earned and I fought for every penny.

It wasn't until I understood that this was a bullshit lie— that it is absolutely possible to be both abundant and generous when empowered with boundaries—that I was able to confidently communicate about contract terms and pricing.

My struggles with worth showed up in my business, but they were rooted in much earlier experiences. Business was just the vehicle through which the wounds became visible. Your own boundary struggles might show up differently than mine, particularly if you don't run your own business; regardless of how they appear in this moment, they are likely rooted in something deeper that you haven't been consciously aware of, until now.

The fact that I can have this conversation publicly while also having a loving relationship with my parents is something I deeply honor about my own healing, about them, and about how our relationship has strengthened as a result of getting these conversations out into the open. I honor how they did better for us than what their own parents did for them. We all screw up at some point in life; we're all likely to hurt someone, knowingly or unknowingly. No matter what parents do for their kids, there is likely something that their kids won't agree with and will be hurt by. It's how we all learn and grow.

I didn't get to this place overnight. That incident with Carrie and her three-minute voicemail was a big first step in recovering my self-worth—but I still had a few pit stops to make along that road.

TOXIC GENEROSITY

Sometimes, I think of lacking boundaries as being like an emotional sponge. Available for purchase anytime, anywhere. Absorbing whatever mess the situation presents, no matter how disgusting, with no reward except that the mess is contained for the moment. Getting used up, over and over again.

If you're cringing, good. Because this is the truth of not having boundaries.

Here's an example. I watched my mother cook and clean like crazy when we were growing up. We had overnight guests nearly every weekend, and while we were extremely grateful for the stream of extended family who came to stay with us (since we never traveled anywhere, we wouldn't have seen them otherwise), I saw what this constant pressure did to my mom. It was a tug-of-war: wanting guests to come, feeling walked all over because having guests is work, resenting the guests for being there, feeling guilty for the resentment ... and by Sunday night, sheer exhaustion.

Why did she do this? I often wondered. What benefit did any of this give her?

She liked having family visit our home. We all did. But she never said no—even when she was tired. Even when she was sick. Even when she just didn't freaking feel like it.

That is what it means to lack boundaries, and to be out of alignment with your soul.

It feels off, but you do it anyway.

You do it because you said you would, not because it makes you happy.

You go along, and don't make waves, all the while seething with resentment because you didn't want this or ask for this but you don't feel like you have a choice.

You "suck it up"—all the emotions, all the anger, all the resistance, all the sadness—because that's what sponges are made to do.

Good lord, that's gross. Let's not do that anymore.

When I kept delivering extra revisions and hours on Carrie's project—even though I felt disrespected and didn't want to continue—I told myself I was being generous, and that my hard work would win out in the end (just like my mom did when she said that if people valued her they'd choose to give her a raise). All the while, I was bubbling with resentment.

That was not generosity. That was *toxic generosity*.

This pattern shows up with our heart-centered clients all the time. They tell me, "I feel bad charging more. I want everyone to be able to afford my services." And so, the pattern plays out. A business owner takes a client at a rate below the one they want (and need to fit their budget goals). They spend hours and energy serving the client. This goes on for weeks, months, sometimes years. The business owner works harder and harder but meanwhile struggles to pay their own bills and misses out on their own family time. They become exhausted, bitter, checked out. They question why they ever got into business in the first place. The situation becomes toxic.

Toxic generosity is the complete opposite to living Unleashed. Toxic generosity says that you are a victim to the things you've agreed to. Unleashed empowers you to speak up and set boundaries in any situation.

You always have a choice.

This doesn't just play out in business situations. Think about a time where you signed up for something because it felt good and generous (volunteer work at your local shelter, the PTO at your kid's school, helping a friend build their new website, whatever). You like it at first, but after a while, it starts to suck up a lot of your time and energy, and it becomes a burden. You start to feel resentment about how much you've taken on. Instead of asking, "Why does everyone need so much from me," or even, "Why the heck did I say yes to this?", what if you asked, "What boundary would need to be in place to make this feel good again?"

CODE-SHIFTING IS ANTITHETICAL TO AUTHENTICITY

If you struggle with boundaries, you may also struggle with code-shifting.

Code-shifting is the act of modifying your speech to adapt to sociocultural norms. And it also commonly means changing your behavior to suit the setting and circumstances. It's the tactic of adjusting your appearance, speech, expressions, communication style, and expressions in order to optimize the comfort of others, in exchange for (you hope) their kind treatment of you. This happens subconsciously for many of us who grew up in traumatic environments, as well as for people of color who are coping with implicit and explicit bias. If we are who people want us to be, our thinking goes, they'll be nicer to us.

Seems logical, right? I mean, given the alternative, why *wouldn't* we tailor our behavior so that people will like us, take care of us, and treat us fairly?

On the surface, you might see code-shifting as no big deal—maybe even an extension of good manners. And there's nothing wrong with subtle adaptation to meet the needs of different life situations. But code-shifting is deeper than that: it's the subversion of our true selves and authentic feelings and desires. That makes it one of the most insidious pieces of conditioning we have to overcome if we want to live in a radically authentic way.

Code-shifting is basically the erasure of boundaries in exchange for safety, love, and acceptance. If you feel like you can't be *you* in any given environment, you will also feel like you can't have boundaries in that environment.

Growing up I was aware of the ways in which I tampered down my true self around different groups of family and friends, but it wasn't until I actively peeled back my own layers of lingering self-shame and self-doubt that I finally realized how much I was squashing my authentic feelings, opinions, and voice. I bent over backwards in order not to "stir the pot" in so many places! My first reaction upon seeing this pattern was to minimize my exposure as much as possible while I figured out how to deal with the rage and shame inside me. That space was much-needed and allowed me to finally determine what was "me," and what was a persona I cultivated in order to gain love and acceptance. (As an aside, I learned that, while avoidance is definitely a good coping mechanism, it's not a permanent solution if you want to live radically authentically and Unleashed.)

Once I came to a place where I could forgive my family, walk the line I'd established with healthy boundaries, did the work to release responsibility and stop code-shifting into the "family counselor" role, I started to have a different relationship with my parents. My mom tells me that she's proud and in awe of the way that I've learned to say no to the things that I don't want in my life, and how I've stepped forward onto a scary, unknown path in pursuit of what *does* feel right for me.

"

IF YOU WANT TO BE REMEMBERED AS SOMEONE WHO HONORED THEIR PATH, YOU HAVE TO START WITH CREATING HEALTHY BOUNDARIES, EVEN WHEN IT MAKES OTHERS WILDLY UNCOMFORTABLE. OTHERWISE, YOU'LL ALWAYS GET PULLED OFF-COURSE.

"

"Does that make me a selfish bitch?" I once asked her.

"Of course not!" she replied. "You're strong. And you inspire me."

As I've done my healing work, my mom has also bene-fited. Our relationship has grown much richer and more joyful, and she's even begun exploring her own bounda-ries in her life. But my reason for doing my healing work isn't because I put my parents first, it's because I put *myself* first. That is what healthy generosity requires.

And my dad? While we don't always see eye-to-eye, and he still doesn't totally understand what I do for work, he definitely wins the prize for Number One Fan (if the amount of bragging he does counts as criteria)! With him, I've come to learn that it is possible to have a deeply lov-ing, meaningful, and even fun relationship with someone who thinks and lives differently than you do—as long as it's supported by good boundaries.

GET SELFISH FOR YOUR SOUL

Imagine that you're at your own end-of-life celebration. You're watching all the important people in your life—significant other(s), friends, family, colleagues, clients, etc.—pay tribute to your time here on Earth.

Are they saying things like, "She was kind, but broken. She gave everything she had for others, but she always put herself last"?

Or, are they saying, "She honored her path. She was so strong. She always did what made her happy. She was an example for me"?

If you're into personal development, you've probably done some version of the above exercise a dozen times. However, what most people don't tell you is that, if you want to be remembered as someone who honored their path, you have to start with creating healthy boundaries, even when it makes others wildly uncomfortable. Otherwise, you'll always get pulled off-course.

Your boundaries are natural extensions of your guiding principles and core values—and when you think of them that way, they become easier to express and stand behind. More, they create safety to step into the "doing" of the Unlocking phase of your Unleashing. By creating healthy, values-aligned boundaries, you can step into the next exciting phase of your life on your own terms.

Looking back, I'm grateful for my experience with my client Carrie, because it showed me where I was being untrue to my values of authenticity, truth, freedom, and badassery. Being authentic and truthful means having empowered conversations with clients as well as with family and friends. It means digging deep into my clients' hopes, dreams, and goals, and helping them create strategies from their souls' guidance. But in order to do that in the way I desire, I need to have *a lot* of confidence in myself and my methods. When I took on Carrie's project, I didn't have that. More, I didn't define the parameters (aka, boundaries) that would set the stage for me to live into the commitments I made.

In order to step into my authentic, badass self in business, I needed to set up a support structure that would help me feel supported in *becoming* her. And when I onboarded my next client, I had a much better framework to keep both my vision and our relationship on track. Sure, it felt a little selfish to lay out my expectations when my client was the one paying for the service—but it made for a much smoother ride in the long run.

CREATING HEALTHY BOUNDARIES

Here's an exercise to help you evaluate your challenges and areas of resistance to see where you might be responding from toxic generosity, and how you can respond from a place of empowered boundaries.

- Step 1: Write out any areas of resistance, or any challenges, that you come up against in your career and relationships.

- Step 2: What is the current response or action you are having? What is that causing to happen?

- Step 3: What alternative response/action can you take that is empowered?

Here's how that could look in a table format:

The area of resistance	What is the response you're having, or the action/inaction you are taking in this situation, and how does that feel?	What is an alternative response/action you can take that's from empowered boundaries? What does that look like?
Example: Every time my best friend calls lately it's to complain about her problems and it's coming up a lot. I feel anxiety and I'm starting to resent her.	I answer because I feel that she needs me. But I feel frustrated because she's not asking me how I'm doing or how I feel. I'm getting frustrated at how I'm expected to be on demand for her problems. The relationship feels one-sided.	*Step 1:* Don't answer when I don't have the capacity or energy to chat. *Step 2:* Let her know how I have been feeling and be honest about what I need in return. *Step 3:* Make an agreement with my friend that we'll check in with each other about if we just need someone to listen, or if we are open to problem-solving. This way I'll know if she wants me to listen so she can vent, or if she wants my help with a solution.

BUILDING UPWARD

Each time you set and hold a boundary, it's like tuning the strings of a guitar. When everything is resonating in attunement with your authentic energy, each action you take will feel like a power chord. And when something is off, you'll just hear it, or feel it.

In this journey to becoming Unleashed, boundaries provide you a beautiful freedom to step into more joy, more expansion. They are an important step to freeing yourself from the leashes of expectation, resentment, and fear. And that's where we're going next—into a world where you live fully free from the leash.

Are you ready?

PART III

UNLEASHED

CHAPTER 7

LIVING OFF THE LEASH

After my trip to Africa with Brandon in 2015 (when I declared my intention to start my business), I had only one challenge before me: actually doing what I'd committed to.

The whisper inside me had grown to a roar, and I trusted my soul awareness enough to know that this leap had become non-negotiable. I was finally going to be me, fully Unleashed in my full authenticity. You can't put a price tag on personal freedom, I told myself. Besides, I had started on a dumpster mattress and worked my way to prodigy status and a six-figure salary in the advertising sales industry. How hard could it be?

Well, as it turns out, *hard.*

The first six weeks were awesome. After breaking away from my hard-earned success and stepping away from my job, I hit the ground running in my new business. By week two I had secured my first client as an independent marketing agency and I didn't even have a live website yet! By week six I had three retainer clients and a baseline revenue. I was running full steam to provide the promised services, while simultaneously learning how to run my business and answer the never-ending stream of questions that popped up from everywhere. It was thrilling.

But as month two drew to a close, the fifteen-hour days and nonstop stream of learning, assimilation, and tasks began to feel overwhelming. In the beginning, the energy of my dream was like rocket fuel; now, that excitement was being drowned out by the rising flood of unknowns and self-doubt that were starting to creep in. There were *so* many questions I simply didn't have answers to. Worse, I was beginning to realize that the tasks I'd agreed to do for my clients were taking way more time than I'd anticipated. Meeting my ambitious sales goals at my current rates simply wouldn't be possible. If I wanted to hire a team, increase my sales, and take the company where I wanted it to go, I wouldn't just need to double my prices. I'd need to increase them by 600 percent.

I started to question my capabilities. My motives. My dream. How had I ever imagined I could be the sole leader of a functioning business?

And yet, from day one, I'd had a vision of something bigger than just me. On my website, I used language like "we" and "us," because I knew building a team was in alignment with my mission and vision.

I started to pay attention to bigger, more successful agencies, and saw that many of them had two or three founders or partners. I started wondering if I had a big ego; was that what had made me think I could build this business on my own?

Now, in addition to all of my other struggles, I started judging myself for "having a big head." I felt like I was a teenager again, being cut down by people for being "too much." But this time the judgment was coming from within myself. Every day, I felt my shoulders slump a little more.

So, I decided to prove to the world (and myself) that I wasn't bitchy and egotistical by doing the "right thing," and finding a business partner. If I found someone to run the agency beside me, it would mean I was leading from the heart, the way I wanted to be, in co-creation with others. I had a deep desire to create a thriving community, a place where people's strengths would be celebrated—and, in my mind, the best way to do that was to get myself and my ego out of the way. Then, we could grow better and stronger, together, with a team.

There was someone in my world who had become a mentor of sorts; we'd gotten to know one another over the past few months, and talked about creating a referral partnership between our businesses. They were further along in their business, and it was clear (to me) that they knew a lot more than I did. It was agreed that this person would join my business as a 50 percent partner.

I was beyond excited. Not only did this feel like a validation of all of my ideas and goals, but since I'd be locking arms with someone who knew more than me in several areas, it would also alleviate a lot of the stress and uncertainty I'd been feeling. Looking back, I think a deep, hidden part of me resented that I'd be, in many ways, taking the position of "second fiddle" when I was meant to be the leader, but I chalked that up to my bruised ego. Besides, this person seemed to be driven and caring, like me, and regularly proclaimed that they were "a person of integrity." Who better to guide me into this next phase of my success?

Turns out, talk is cheap.

JOY OVER JUDGMENT

My business partnership was formed, evolved, and imploded in just under four months.

It seems like such a short time, looking back. But, like earthquakes, tornadoes, and volcanic eruptions, sometimes the most intense and devastating situations happen in a heartbeat—and leave a trail of destruction that can take months, or even years, to clean up.

Yes, it was *that* bad.

The truth was, this partnership was perfectly aligned for me, but not in the way I imagined. It wasn't aligned to my values, my vision, or even my goals. It wasn't aligned to who I am, or even who I was at that time. It was, however, a beautiful fit for my limiting beliefs.

From the moment I started considering a partnership, my inner knowing knew something was *way* off. I remember feeling that core-deep discomfort about the situation, but it was quickly muted by my imposter syndrome, which by this point was playing on full blast. Every question I asked, every problem I tried to solve, was being filtered through that energy. When I brought my partner in, they only reinforced my fear that I was incompetent, inexperienced, and underprepared.

Alarm bells were constantly going off in my heart, but they didn't feel like truth. They felt like shame. Shame for "not being enough." That feeling of shame only seemed to confirm the messages I was hearing from my inner critic.

It wasn't one single thing that finally woke me up to the fact that I needed to dissolve the partnership. It was a million individual violations to my soul awareness. I knew that starting a business would be stressful, but the vortex I was in with the partnership went way beyond business stress. It felt like constant emotional whiplash, topped with a fair amount of gaslighting. By this point, I was even more filled with self-doubt than I had been when I decided I needed a partner. I was terrified of losing my clients, my income, and my reputation. I had started my business through intentionally built relationships; how could these people ever trust me again, when I couldn't even trust myself to make the most important decisions in my business life?

Even more painful were the negative stories and outright lies my former partner was spreading about me in our local business community. It was devastating to be painted as something I was not, and shattered what little confidence I had left. But as tempting as it was to set the record straight, something in me held strong and refused to feed into it. I was done with that kind of toxicity in my business.

I had gone into business for myself so I could live Unleashed. And yet, the moment I stepped into the freedom I'd always claimed to want, I choked. Now, my internal landscape was shredded and scarred, but a kernel of soul awareness still glimmered; this kept my spirit alive enough to trust my next steps, despite my devastating imposter syndrome.

There was a huge lesson here, I realized. While I couldn't go back and do the last few months again, I had a choice about where to go from here. I could keep myself trapped

"I NEEDED TO LIVE IN MY TRUTH AND ATTRACT THE PEOPLE WHO ALIGNED WITH IT, NOT TRY TO BUILD MY TRUTH INTO THE CRACKS OF AN "ACCEPTABLE" STRUCTURE."

in negativity, drama, and self-doubt, or I could claim my authentic power and move forward in a new way.

The truth was, I'd always known *exactly* what to do to build the business I desired. I was just too scared to do it. I was too afraid of what—and who—I'd leave behind, by being "too big," or "too bold." I was still waiting for permission—not from my family, this time, but from a community of clients and colleagues whose respect (and business) I desired. But if I wanted them to acknowledge and believe in the real me—in me as I truly was—I needed to show up that way first. I needed to live in my truth and attract the people who aligned with it, not try to build my truth into the cracks of an "acceptable" structure.

Shakily, I chose truth over fear.

But more, I chose joy over judgment.

From that point forward, I put all of my focus toward alignment with my truth and finding joy and gratitude for every task I "got the privilege to do" to move my business forward. I focused on deeds, not words. My mission was no longer to meet a numerical goal, but to serve each client fully, one at a time, as I knew that would lead to the numbers. I may have gotten into "business bed" with the wrong person, but I didn't have to lay there feeling guilty. I could swing the pendulum to the other side, and deliver from a place of truth, clarity, and integrity.

The joy of taking control of the situation moved me past not only the judgment of my former business partner, but my own judgment of myself.

THE IMPOSTER SYNDROME FILTER

Up until this point, we've worked with uncovering your truth and unlocking your authenticity in a way that feels aligned for you.

You know who you are. You know what you value. You know how and why you want to live Unleashed.

So why are you still looking through the lens of an imposter?

The truth is, you can filter your experience through many energetic lenses. Your experiences and beliefs will always color the way you receive information about yourself and the world. However, when you step onto your personal stage and start living Unleashed, you become empowered with a unique ability: to *filter your decisions through your authenticity*, and use your personal truth as the metric by which all of your choices are measured.

Authentic power is healthy. It allows you to make decisions that are in everyone's highest good—including yours. It's the *only* path to building an Unleashed life and a business that supports it.

Imposter syndrome is the evil twin of authentic power. It will paint your authentic urges as "ego," "self-delusion," or just "having a big head." It will say, "Don't believe in yourself *that* much. Who do you think you are?"

Interestingly, the more capable we are, and the closer we get to the center of our authentic power, the more imposter syndrome will try to steal the show.

A few years ago, I learned about something called the Dunning–Kruger effect, in which people with low ability at a task predictably overestimate their own ability. The more experience they gain at their chosen task over time, the more that their confidence drops to a level on par with their ability. On the opposite end of the spectrum, researchers say, the reverse is true: high performers, as a group, tend to underestimate their skills and struggle with self-doubt.

When our skill is high, but our confidence is low, what happens is a kind of reverse Dunning–Kruger effect—otherwise known as imposter syndrome.

When I made the misaligned decision to bring in a business partner, I was definitely bottoming out on the confidence curve. I was already a skilled brand strategist, a good marketer, and a capable leader, but the overwhelm of my new venture thrust me into self-sabotage.

In my experience, most heart-centered visionaries and creatives experience imposter syndrome at some point. That feeling of inadequacy is almost always strongest when they are stepping into something aligned with their authenticity.

There are many reasons for this, but I think the two biggest are the following.

One, when you are building an Unleashed life and business perfectly created for you, there is no exact model to follow. What is right for you may be radically different than anything the world has seen before—and because it looks so different, it's tempting to make it wrong.

Two, when you're doing what is authentically aligned for you, it will feel easy. And, since many of us are conditioned to think that "easy" means "too good to be true"—and, conversely, that nothing is worth having or achieving unless it's bone-grindingly hard—we sell ourselves short. This doesn't mean that every part of change is easy, only that the parts that are super soul-aligned will flow with ease.

Both of these detours will send us straight down the road to Imposter Land, if we're not aware of them.

The solution to imposter syndrome is actually simple, if not always easy to implement. Basically, it's to let your joy be bigger than your judgment, and use everything in your toolbox (including your RAD Badass List and the other tools in this book) to inflate your self-confidence to a level on par with your actual skills and abilities.

If you care about living Unleashed—and making a positive impact in the world at the same time—confidence is your biggest asset. I knew, when I started my business, that being in alignment with my soul mission would require me to become much bigger—in all ways—than who I was currently being. At the same time, I mistakenly believed that in order to become "big," without being a bitch or walking all over everyone, I needed to shove my ego in a box and give my power away.

Your true path to living Unleashed will require you to grow and trust yourself in ways you never imagined before. But it will *never* require you to make yourself smaller.

LEAD YOURSELF BEFORE YOU LEAD OTHERS

For many of us who are called to live authentically and create something bigger than ourselves, leadership is a big part of our journey. Whether we're ready to claim that or not, it often comes with the territory for visionaries, or anyone who desires to grow and advance in life.

Before we can lead anyone, however, we need to learn how to lead ourselves.

When I say "lead yourself," I don't mean ratcheting up your self-discipline and tightening the leash of self-judgment and limiting beliefs to give yourself some illusion of control. You're done with that. Instead, it's the opposite: once you get clear on what living Unleashed looks like for you, your biggest task is to *lead yourself toward that vision*—whatever it takes. That's what living off the leash really means.

How often have you felt a desire, or dreamed a dream, but you cut yourself short before you even allowed yourself to explore what was possible? How often do you judge yourself into paralysis before you take a single action? I see this happen with my clients every day, both in micro-judgments they hardly notice—like saying, "Ooh, I *should* do that," or "I feel bad that I screwed up and am feeling off today"—and in macro-judgments—like thinking, "I'm too bossy," or, "If I was only X, things would be so much better."

Judgment is the biggest killer of joy. And joy is essential for living Unleashed.

The solution isn't to make yourself wrong for making judgments—untying yourself from that knot is practically impossible—but to replace judgment with curiosity.

My client Melissa came to me with a goal of earning a *lot* more money, and the pain of feeling like she was constantly selling herself short. Like most clients I work with, what she really desired wasn't just money; it was to be free to be more of who she was, in every way.

When we started working together, Melissa was already outwardly successful, leading a therapy practice with a staff of twenty (and growing) and annual revenues in the neighborhood of $1 million. She had written a book, hosted a podcast, and seemed to have fun in whatever she chose to do. But she also had a vision beyond her current reality. She felt like she had outgrown her identity as a therapist, but couldn't picture what actually came next. More money, she reasoned, would give her the "safety" to explore this new identity and claim it.

Complicating matters was the fact that Melissa's business wasn't as profitable as it could be. It looked good from the outside, but it was heavily in debt, and the constant hustling to keep it above water left Melissa feeling trapped. Her marriage wasn't exactly thriving, either. While neither was actively failing, and her status quo might have been more than "good enough" for some, it wasn't the reality that allowed her to be *all* of her.

So, we set out to discover what the "Unleashed" Melissa looked like.

We found a Melissa who is playful, introverted, and requires daily naps to restore her energy. A Melissa who believes in coaching but held back on offering coaching to clients because being a therapist felt safer and more "credentialed." A Melissa who lives with bi-polar disorder, who is an artist, and who is an LGBTQIA ally and educator.

Most importantly, we found a Melissa who can be all of these things, simultaneously, without apology.

Our shared mission became supporting the transformation that would allow Melissa to align with, step into, and fully unleash her most authentic self. When she found a path to doing that, she would also find the money and freedom she desired.

Despite a difficult childhood and many obstacles along the way, Melissa had an incredible RAD Badass List. Her spunky personality, sheer determination, and grit pulled her through some difficult situations, and she was proud of herself for coming as far as she had. When combined with what we learned from her unique Human Design, Strengths, and Motivators (third-party assessments we encourage all of our clients to participate in to gain new awareness about their internal landscapes), she was able to shift her self-view and lean into her natural authority. More, they allowed her to get curious about who she was and who she wanted to be, instead of shaming herself for what she saw as deficiencies. For example, instead of shaming herself for being a multi-creative and being "unable" to focus on just one thing, she began to see how her work as an artist and activist actually fueled her across all of her various roles and identities.

A few months in, as we entered the Unlocking phase of our work (the part where things often start to feel "grindy" and we want to run for the safety of the sameness we've known for so long), Melissa reached a point of resistance. As we were discussing business financials, staff roles, and profit margins, I noticed that it simply wouldn't be possible for Melissa to work less and step into greater freedom without transforming the way that she was operating in her day-to-day work life.

I began asking questions about specific staff roles and responsibilities. Some of the staff weren't performing their responsibilities to the fullest. But when it came to actually having conversations about accountability, Melissa was struggling.

We created some strategies, and Melissa set about having those difficult conversations. To her credit, she actually did it—but a few weeks later, the same issues were still there. I invited her to drop her self-judgment and get curious about why she might not be holding her staff accountable.

What came through was a limiting belief that had been keeping Melissa in a cycle of overwork and low profitability: *"I'm not smart enough to lead."*

Here was a woman who had survived and thrived despite a difficult childhood, who was the first in her family to go to college, who had built a business that more than twenty people made the conscious choice to join as staff, who had changed lives as a school social worker whose students adored her and still kept in touch with her years later ... and she still held on to this belief that she wasn't smart enough to lead her business.

What unfolded from there was an unraveling of painful past experiences that had led Melissa to carry unfounded judgments about herself. Like the time when she'd sought guidance from a school counselor about college options, but was blown off with a curt, "I didn't think you'd be going to college." That one moment created a self-judgment that held her back for years. Melissa built her company and team, but all the while, she was holding back from asking for the support she really needed from her team, because she believed the lie that she wasn't smart enough to show them the way. And, just as her guidance counselor had overlooked her skills and intelligence, so too was she overlooking her own capabilities.

The truth is, Melissa is more than capable of leading a successful team and business. But an unconscious choice to believe a false story about herself and her abilities was simply standing in the way of that success.

With her self-judgment cleared, Melissa was able to go back and have empowering, productive conversations with her staff. She gave clearer boundaries so everyone knew what was expected of them. With better support, Melissa was able to step into the role of a visionary leader. She dropped her judgments, Unleashed her true self, and fully claimed the success she desired and deserved.

In the short term, Melissa got back five whole days a month in her schedule to pursue the things that lit her up from the inside. Twelve months in, she had cleared out nearly $100,000 in business debt, tripled her personal income, and cut her workweek to ten hours or less so that she could launch her new business focused on coaching, retreats, and selling art. She uncoupled from a marriage that was no longer fulfilling, purchased land in Puerto Rico, and is now building properties to host retreats.

All this because she chose to drop her judgment, get curious, open herself to new awarenesses, and follow her joy.

That, my friend, is living Unleashed.

So, as you step into true freedom and alignment in your own journey, let me ask you: Where can you get curious? Where can you drop your self-judgment, rachet up your confidence, and reverse your imposter syndrome by remembering your badass-ness? Where can you become a more powerful leader of *you?*

DISCOVERING YOUR GENIUS

One of my favorite books is *The Big Leap: Conquer Your Hidden Fear and Take Life to the Next Level*, by Gay Hendricks. In it, the author suggests that we all have a zone of incompetence, a zone of competence, a zone of excellence, and a zone of genius.

Your zone of incompetence includes the things, tools, and tasks that you aren't gifted or comfortable in. It feels hard to do those tasks or move through life in those ways. The zone of competence covers things you can do moderately well, but don't enjoy and aren't great at. The zone of excellence includes the things or ways of being that you are really skilled at—the things that everyone asks you to help them with, or the things you've built your career around.

But the final layer—the deepest layer—is your zone of genius. When you work from your zone of genius, you're capitalizing on your natural, innate abilities, rather than just behaviors and tools you've learned. I think of this as working from your authenticity. In practice, it feels like flow, joy, and ease; it's a sweet spot at the intersection of who you authentically are, what you are skilled at, and what brings you joy.

When you uncover, unlock, and step fully into living in and leading from your zone of genius, you become fully Unleashed.

This doesn't just apply in your work life (although I would argue that it's hard to live Unleashed while you're working a job that doesn't overlap in at least some ways with your zone of genius.) In fact, when I was sharing this with a friend recently, she paused.

"I get the application to career," she said thoughtfully. "But how would I apply this to my current phase of life, which is focused on parenting and homemaking?"

"What do you think your zone of genius is?" I asked her.

"Definitely my creativity. I can turn anything into an art project."

"And ... can you do that in parenting?" I asked. (Having chosen not to have kids myself, I'm not an expert in this sort of stuff.) "Can you make even the mundane daily stuff—like washing bottles and wiping butts—feel creative and aligned with who you are?"

"I think I need to find a way," my friend said.

And she has. Her home is filled to the brim with beautiful, bright, eclectic art that she makes with her kids out of everything from eggshells to acorns to old cardboard boxes. Her whole home practically oozes fun, laughter, and learning. And, even as she's indulging her passion, she's leading her kids to become creative thinkers in their own right.

Of course, there's a margin of realism—no one, in any life situation, is going to love and be an expert at everything they need to do, every day, all the time—but we all can look for opportunities to infuse our zone of genius into everyday tasks. This will not only bring us more joy, it will fill up your cup so you can more easily muscle through the stuff you don't love as much.

The more I've optimized my work, music, and relationships to spend more time in my zone of genius, the happier I am, the better I lead, and the more sustainable living Unleashed becomes. Because I'm no longer busy trying to do the things I'm merely competent at, I have more time for what really matters.

In our Soul Seed Strategy coaching programs, we ask clients to run a two-week Zone of Genius Time and Energy study. Here's how it goes:

- Step 1: Keep track of all of your personal and business tasks and activities for two weeks.

- Step 2: Track how much time goes into each task.

- Step 3: Track how much energy goes into each task, what fills you up, and what depletes you. What do you look forward to? What do you dread? Where do you notice your best flow and productivity?

"IF YOU ARE SPREADING YOURSELF THIN AND DOING ALL THE THINGS, ALL THE TIME—EVEN IF YOU'RE DOING THEM INSIDE AN ALIGNED MODEL—YOU ARE LIVING WITH BLINDERS ON AND ONCE AGAIN EXHAUSTING YOURSELF WITH "SHOULDS.""

This exercise will give you lots of great information to work with. You'll get to see what you are actually doing, and how it aligns with your core values. You'll also see where you're just plain wasting your time, and where you can easily ask for support with mundane tasks that are impeding your flow.

The trend I see, having done this with dozens of clients, is that we focus most on the things that are hard for us, saving our best work for the times when we have nothing left in the tank. By flipping this and creating new structures, we are able to be more creative, less reactive, and more accountable to our goals and dreams.

What does this have to do with living Unleashed?

Everything.

Just like you can't create an Unleashed life without strong boundaries, you can't savor the freedom of living Unleashed—and capitalize on it for your growth, joy, and leadership—if you have no time or space to breathe. If you are spreading yourself thin and doing all the things, all the time—even if you're doing them inside an aligned model—you are living with blinders on and once again exhausting yourself with "shoulds." Identifying your zone of genius shows you where you can (and *must*) ask for help so you can get out there and actually *live* the badass life you're creating.

My first five years in business, I felt like I was constantly chasing my tail ... but I learned by doing what to keep on my plate and what not to. Learning to delegate brought so much relief. More, it brought spaciousness. Now, I enjoy many more lazy mornings with my pups and gig runs with my band—and my business is better than ever. It's in nobody's best interest for me to do all the things. And it's in everyone's best interest for me to be in my zone of genius.

On the flip side, it's possible to get *too* comfortable in your zone of genius. I see this happen to many clients: they do well for a while, but then they get bored or complacent and decide to try something else. Or, they trigger themselves into self-sabotage because it feels "too easy"—which, of course, means something must be wrong. In these cases, rather than find a new challenge to reignite their passion and creativity, they blow up their entire lives and businesses thinking that they need to "start over." When this happens, they often end up working outside their zones of genius, and dropping all the lessons that being *in* the zone taught them about living Unleashed.

By all means, blow it up if you must. But let the explosion carry you toward something better, not something lesser. Or, better yet, don't burn it down at all—just in case, after you test those newer, greener pastures, you decide you want to come back.

RUNNING FREE

Getting yourself off the leash isn't always the biggest challenge. It's keeping yourself there that really blows you open!

Where you're headed next is likely to poke at all of your old programming at first—but once you try it for yourself, you'll know there's no going back. You just need to keep tapping into your zone of genius, put one foot in front of the other, and put progress before perfection.

CHAPTER 8

PROGRESS OVER PERFECTIION

A few years into my business journey, I started offering group and one-on-one coaching to help others learn to grow their businesses through solid brand strategy and empowered leadership. Early on in my coaching days, I dedicated *a lot* of time to the consultation process, meeting with prospective clients multiple times and basically giving away a ton of free strategy in an effort to prove I was "worth" what I was (eventually) going to ask them to pay me. By the time someone actually plunked down their credit card, I reasoned, they'd have a taste of what they could expect when we started working together.

One of those prospective clients, a woman I'll call Bree, wasn't ready to invest in coaching after the first three meetings, but we kept in touch. Several months later, just before the Christmas holiday, she contacted me to say that she was ready to make the leap from solopreneur to CEO in her business and wanted to hire me to assist with that transition. She hoped to receive some prep materials from me before the holiday break so she could get a jumpstart on our work, which would begin in the new year.

Sometimes, people aren't ready until they're ready—and I was thrilled that the time I'd spent with Bree earlier in the year had paid off.

By this point in my business journey, I rarely took on work without a paid deposit, because I knew it was not in anyone's best interest for me to work for free (even if I was still giving away free coaching and consulting disguised as sales calls). But in this case, I decided to make an exception, and spent that Friday evening and several hours over the weekend preparing a customized workbook to support Bree's individual goals and needs. I had a good grasp on where she wanted to go and what was blocking her from getting there from the hours of free consulting I'd already provided.

In the end, I sent her about fifteen pages of materials that would help her dive in before our first session. Feeling proud of myself, and excited for the growth that was about to unfold for both Bree and me, I sat back to enjoy the rest of my holiday.

A week later, Bree still hadn't paid her deposit, which was weird since she'd promised to send it immediately. I emailed her to find out what was happening. What I received back wasn't an update on payment status, or even a note of thanks for giving up my holiday weekend to prep her materials. It wasn't even, "Hey, thanks, but I've changed my mind."

Instead, my mouth dropped open as I read a scathing email about the grammatical errors in the materials I'd prepared—including a statement that she "couldn't possibly work with someone who didn't value basic business skills like copywriting."

Were there some errors in the workbook? Sure. But they weren't numerous or substantial enough to detract from what was being presented. And I'd written the damn thing in a weekend!

The feeling in my body was the same as that time when Carrie left me that scathing voicemail about how she expected more from me, even though I'd already gone beyond our scope. This was a similar situation: I knew I'd done good work, but Bree was refusing to see or acknowledge it—even after I'd broken my own boundary by attempting to serve her without collecting the deposit first.

As crappy as this felt, after a few breaths (and a few moments of righteous fuming), I was able to step back and see that this had nothing at all to do with me. My only true error had been not invoicing Bree before I sent over the materials.

Bree had hired me to help her overcome the blocks that were preventing her from growing a functioning team and expanding her business beyond a one-person show. Perfectionism was one of the blocks I had intended to help her navigate, once we got deeper into our work. The truth was, my typos had triggered her, and her response showed me that she simply wasn't ready to work with me. We weren't a match.

More, I felt at peace with respecting her point of view. Her truth was hers, and mine was mine, and neither of us needed to be right or wrong. By that point I had had dozens of successes; I knew the value we provided in our containers of work. I had watched many of our clients learn new ways to communicate so they could double and triple their rates, and go from being unhappy in unfulfilling careers to replacing their income (and more) in their new businesses. Some had even increased their revenue by a factor of ten in under a year by engaging our strategic guidance.

"WHEN YOU'RE LIVING UNLEASHED, IT'S VITAL TO SET CLEAR EXPECTATIONS FOR YOURSELF WHILE ALSO EMBRACING THE ACT OF PROGRESS OVER PERFECTION. OTHERWISE, YOU'LL "SHOULD" YOURSELF RIGHT OUT OF YOUR DREAMS."

None of those results required perfect grammar from me.

Had I been selling copywriting services to Bree, her response would have made sense, but that wasn't what I was selling—and it's not what she was buying, either.

I was able to respond calmly and with clarity to Bree's message, and by the time that conversation was done, I felt proud of myself. My actions hadn't been "perfect" in this situation—in particular, I'd ignored my own boundaries, *again*—but in the end, I learned something profound, and I knew I would do better next time.

After Bree, I revised our consult syntax to help guide clients to get even more present to their own transformation, and to what that transformation would actually require. Our sales process was no longer just about the client saying yes to a scope of work, it was about helping them become aware and committed to the internal transformation that would inevitably be required in order for any new strategy to work. That way, both of us could see if it was truly an aligned fit for us to support their efforts. Progress!

I also reconsidered how I was creating client materials. If I hadn't been in such a rush to meet Bree's deadline, I would have reviewed things more thoroughly—not to make them "perfect," but to ensure that they met the standards we strive for. An energy of quality is different from perfectionism—and I get to be clear about which energy I'm playing in. Progress!

Today, after having worked with hundreds of business owners around the world, I can absolutely speak to the importance of setting expectations as best you can, even as you are embracing progress and learning as you go. It's natural for things to get sticky when we're in a process of growth or change, so don't worry about needing to have everything perfect. Set the expectation as best you can, but don't get trapped by shaming yourself when things don't go to plan. Mistakes happen as you are learning and growing—and as those mistakes happen, nobody needs to be made wrong in it.

Often, it's easier for people to judge and assign blame than it is to lean into discomfort and get curious about it and see what learning is there for them—as was the case with Bree. The old me would've felt guilty and battled self-doubt over Bree's finger-pointing. But you no longer need to let other people's projections scare you back to perfection. Their need for control and certainty (aka, perfectionism) is likely what is keeping them stuck. Don't let it keep you stuck, too.

This doesn't just apply to client situations. When you're living Unleashed, it's vital to set clear expectations for yourself while also embracing the act of progress over perfection. Otherwise, you'll "should" yourself right out of your dreams.

YOU DON'T ALWAYS NEED TO GET IT RIGHT

When you begin to lean into your authenticity, you will find yourself repeating certain key lessons and situations over and over again. It's like your growth unfolds in an upward spiral, bringing you back to the same place over and over, only at a different level, so you can learn the lesson again from a different vantage point.

This is what happened to me with Bree. It was essentially the same situation that had unfolded with Carrie years earlier; both occurred because I put my desire to please ahead of my boundaries, and didn't create clarity around expectations. But the experiences themselves—and the feelings I felt around them—were vastly different because of the progress I had made in the meantime.

By all means, strive for excellence. Excellence is different than perfection. It includes permission for you to thrive, without the unrealistic demands of "perfect."

But ... how do you define "excellence"?

For that matter, how do you define "Unleashed"?

The answer is *clear expectations*.

When things show up that we don't like or don't make us feel good, it's an opportunity—to choose differently, to shift something, to let go, to do more of something.

It's up to you to set the parameters, tone, and benchmarks for your own growth. Seeing everything as an opportunity to make progress allows you to stay curious and fluid enough to try new things, while engaging with your challenges through an empowered filter (rather than an "imposter" filter). When you expect to learn from everything, you no longer have to get down on yourself or call yourself a screwup if you lose a lucrative client over a few spelling errors. Instead, you can see the lesson, and keep moving up the growth spiral toward your goals.

Regardless of how this looks in your life, one thing is always true. You *only* learn by doing—and that requires doing the damn thing, not overthinking it in pursuit of perfection.

As true a mantra as "progress over perfection" has been for me in business, it's been doubly true in the music world.

When most people picture life in a rock band, they imagine glamorous dressing rooms, over-the-top costumes, bright lights, and killer dance moves. They see Lzzy Hale owning the guitar riffs, and Gwen Stefani leaping around the stage like a ninja.

What they don't imagine is five people riding on a cheap float in a small-town parade. And yet, that's where Brandon and I got our start.

In those early dumpster-diving days, I *really* wanted us to get hired for gigs, so I networked with people I knew and started talking us up. Pretty soon, I got us a line for a gig at the county fair!

"It would be great to have you ride on our fair float during the holiday parade and play some songs to promote your gig at the fair," the organizer said.

"YOU ONLY LEARN BY DOING—AND THAT REQUIRES DOING THE DAMN THING, NOT OVERTHINKING IT IN PURSUIT OF PERFECTION."

I was beyond excited. This was going to be our big debut to the community, including many of our friends and family! I had a vision of us rocking our way down the main drag on a big rig, the beat of our music pulsing through the streets.

Well, sometimes the vision doesn't match the reality.

We were set up on the back of a hay wagon with a tiny PA system hooked up to a portable generator. Things were going ... okay, at first, but halfway through the parade the generator failed and started spurting oil all over Brandon.

I started making jokes over the mic. "Hey, Brandon, we can't hear you! Turn it up, babe!" Little did I know that the generator was on the verge of exploding. I kept singing, unaccompanied, only half-aware that my mic wasn't working, until I finally stuttered to a halt.

People along the parade route watched us, confused, as our five-piece band rolled by, with four of us standing there in total mortification while our drummer kept going with a very long, very awkward drum solo.

As if that wasn't bad enough ...

A month later, at the county fair, we played the "real" gig we'd been hired for. Or, tried to. All of the bandmates had different visions for what the band should be, but instead of working it out and creating a sound, we all just kind of ... did our own thing. Our bassist insisted on playing a three-minute Beavis and Butthead intro over the speaker system (he thought this was hilarious, but the wholesome farm families in the audience were confused, to say the least). Our drummer played completely to his own beat, which he made up as he went along and changed multiple times within the same song.

When at last it was over, Brandon and I flew out of there and declared that we would never again put ourselves in a situation like this, with five people in conflict on the stage for everyone to see. Progress!

Then, there was the time when we played at a biker party and one of my friends started texting everyone to tell them how bad we were (we weren't stellar, but we were pretty good for our genre, and for the measly pay. You get what you pay for!). Another woman, a friend of my mom's, told the bar in the neighboring town not to hire us.

Brandon and I agreed: don't invite people to gigs who don't like metal music. Progress!

Later, after forming and dissolving several bands, we founded Morningstar. My baby brother Dave joined us as drummer, and it became a tight-knit family affair. Between Brandon, Dave, and myself, with our shared commitment to the band, we started actually getting good. To solve the issue of finding aligned band members, Brandon started pre-recording the bass and rhythm guitar parts, and streaming them through the speakers at our live shows.

One night, we were opening for a well-known touring band at an outdoor festival. During our set, the sound kept cutting out. I tried to make jokes about it and keep the audience engaged while we waited for the sound crew to fix it so that we could continue our set, but it was almost as awkward as the parade float episode.

As soon as our set wrapped up, the lead sound guy came up and started screaming in my face. I hadn't even taken a step off the stage before he let loose on me, calling me names and putting all of us down on a personal level. I had never felt so attacked in my life. I was shocked, trembling, and crying, and all the while this jerk was calling me a bitch and blaming me for the equipment failures.

Turns out, the venue was trying to run all the sound on a puny generator (sound familiar?) and the same issues happened for the headlining band, too. The guy never apologized, and while I was really shaken for a while, thankfully I had Brandon and other great people to remind me of my RAD Badass list and all the other trolls I'd survived in our earlier years. I decided to block the guy on social media, as ultimately he didn't matter in my life; with that boundary in place, I was able to move forward and bounce back in my shine. My joy and purpose were bigger than some random dude's toxic behavior. They had to be—otherwise, what the hell was I even doing?

Crap like this is enough to make anyone want to quit the industry—and it happens all the time, particularly to women. Some people in the music business (some men, in particular) don't like it when I speak up for myself. They don't like it when I refuse to take part in their misogynistic bullshit. They've labeled me bitchy, bossy, a diva, and untalented. They've called me fat and spread rumors that I was pregnant when we parted ways with them for sub-par work in the band. Before I was Unleashed, this kind of stuff almost took me down so many times.

Women ask me all the time how I survived it. My answer is always, "Progress over perfection"—and also one of my favorite AC/DC lyrics: "It's a long way to the top / if you wanna rock-n-roll!" I've never been perfect, but rock-n-roll isn't about perfection. If I learned enough to do better next time, I've rocked the day—even if I end up singing into a dead mic while covered in hay and gasoline.

START BEFORE YOU FEEL READY

If a friend told you about how they showed up on the first day of their new job and their employer didn't have a desk or computer for them, you might tell your friend to start looking for other jobs. Am I right?

Well, that employer was me!

As a new business owner, I honestly had no idea how to hire someone. But I knew I needed help, and I had a vision for how to use that help. And so, my new hire showed up to our small, bare-bones co-working space to find that I literally had nowhere for her to sit and no computer for her to work on.

I'm so grateful she didn't run screaming. In fact, she stayed for more than two years—and when she left, it was to open her own business.

I've always been one to move before I felt ready. I started a business before I had any guarantee of success and created a million-dollar company. I hired my first employees without knowing what contracts or legal paperwork were needed, and eventually created a standout work environment that people seek out and are proud to be part of. As a kid, I started bowling with bumpers on the lanes because my aim was so bad, and eventually went on to win tournaments. I started off in a band whose members could barely play in time with one another and ended up fronting Morningstar.

If I had waited until I was "ready" to do any of those things ... well, I'm glad that I don't know the answer to that. I certainly wouldn't be living Unleashed.

The same is true for you. If you had waited until you were "ready" to take action in your own life, you wouldn't have that awesome RAD Badass list sitting in your notebook right now.

The truth is, you will *never* be ready to take your next big step into living Unleashed. The level of authenticity and truth you're after can't be created until you actually do the thing you know comes next.

So, as you move into this new way of being in your life, don't let your fear of the unknown hold you back. Moving forward into the unknown is messy and scary—but messy is better than nothing, and scared is better than stuck.

MESSY GETS YOU STARTED

You don't need to live your whole life in a scary mess in order to be Unleashed. In fact, there will be times in your journey where "messy" may cause you more problems than you need. When I hired my first employee, I learned as I went. But if I'd kept hiring without onboarding processes and systems in place, it would have been chaos.

Messy gets you started—but eventually, you are going to want more order so your life can grow and flow. You will learn to make quicker, more aligned decisions from your guiding principles and core values. You will learn to savor the mess, while at the same time planning for the next level of order.

And then, there will be the times when you want to throw your hands in the air and say, "Screw it all!"

To bridge this gap with grace, I recommend something I call my "one night rule." When I hit a threshold—when I feel like life is piling on too much, too fast—I give myself one night to wallow with chocolate and Netflix. But the next morning? It's a new day, and it's time for me to step up as an even more Unleashed version of me. If I find myself at "threshold" more than once every few weeks, that's my indicator to reevaluate what I'm doing on a larger scale because somewhere, something is off.

The more practice you have at being the authentic you, the easier it becomes to start before you are ready, take the lessons from the mess, and claim the next stage of your life. It may never be perfect, and you may never feel fully ready—but babe, if you wanted perfect, you'd be standing on the sidelines in a tidy little bubble, not out on the stage living Unleashed and rocking your heart out.

CELEBRATE ALONG THE WAY

On a group call in one of my programs, we were celebrating my client, Leila, who had completed our program and was moving on from the container. I invited her to share her biggest celebrations from our nine months in working together and her intentions for the year ahead.

"I need to use the budget tracker so my sales can improve," she said.

Leila had come into coaching with inconsistent revenue, which is quite common for many service-based businesses in the first few years. There were some months of no to low billing, and as much as $1,200 in others. Her long-term goal was to build a consistent six-figure revenue and hire a team. She also had dreams of becoming a parent, and wanted to create her business in such a way that it could continue to function while she took time off for maternity leave at some point in the future.

Over our year together, Leila learned how to use the proactive budget tracker that we provide to our clients. She shifted from being reactive to proactive with sales, and stepped into more empowered money management practices. She went from inconsistent $1,000 months to consistent $5,000–$6,000 months, and was well on her way to $10,000 months.

In light of this, her share that she "needed to do better" came as a surprise to me.

I invited her to consider that she had more than tripled her sales in the last few months, and asked her how that felt. Instantly, her tune changed. She'd been so focused on making progress, doing the work, and stepping into her Unleashed life and business that she'd forgotten how far she'd come.

Progress will pay off. But it can start to feel like a grind if you don't stop once in a while to look back and appreciate where that incremental progress has carried you.

In 2016, I beta tested my first offer: a four-week small group coaching container for $250. I wasn't sure what people would think of it, or if it was any good. I had a constant feeling that I wasn't delivering enough. Fewer than half of the people who enrolled showed up most weeks—and, since only six had signed up in total, that meant I was pouring my all into two or three people each week. By week four, I was feeling exhausted and questioning if it was all worth it.

Then, the testimonials started to come in.

I was blown away. Even the people who had only made it to one or two live calls spoke about how powerful the course was for them. One participant even declared it "life-changing."

To this day, in moments of self-doubt, I go back to that piece of feedback that someone had a life-changing experience in a program that I was worried was total crap.

"MOVING FORWARD INTO THE UNKNOWN IS MESSY AND SCARY—BUT MESSY IS BETTER THAN NOTHING, AND SCARED IS BETTER THAN STUCK."

(It's on my RAD Badass List.) No matter how much I grow or how confident I become, there are moments when the next step seems like an impossible leap. Revisiting my successes reminds me of what "progress over perfection" made possible—not just for me, but for others, too.

The content I taught in that first program for $250 has become the bedrock of much of my work, and in less than five years has grown into a $30,000/year offer that is designed to help clients make significant strategic growth strides in their own businesses. Progress over perfection made that possible.

I've delivered full-scale webinars to two or three people. I've played to empty rooms. I've lost employees and clients and dealt with all kinds of setbacks. And every time, even if I couldn't see it at the time, these experiences moved me forward. Even when I didn't think people were listening. Even when I couldn't see the support I had.

So, celebrate the fact that you made that first pitch, made that first hire, played that first gig, spoke on stage that first time, bought that first outrageous outfit, booked that first retreat, entered that first pageant, or started that first business. And, celebrate the fact that you made that first mistake, let go of a team member despite how painful it was, bombed that one gig, fell down on stage that one time, rocked that wardrobe malfunction, survived that crazy trip, or failed with that first business partnership. Remember that all of it is worth celebrating, because all of it—the highs and the lows, the wins and the lessons—are what living Unleashed requires.

LIVING IN PROGRESS

Over time, progress over perfection goes from being a simple, proactive approach to an empowered way of living. This isn't just about achieving goals (although that's fun); it's about you leading the way in your Unleashed life.

So, ask yourself now: "What have I been avoiding?"

Or, better yet: "Where in my life have I been waiting to feel 'ready' before moving forward?"

Chances are, there's a step you know you want to take to live off the leash that is simultaneously exciting and dread-inducing. Maybe there's a boundary that needs to be communicated, or something that needs to be released. Or, maybe there's an opportunity that you know is meant for you, but you're scared to put yourself forward.

Right now, answer the following questions:

- Where in my life do I feel resentful, or like a victim?
- What am I resisting?
- What would it take for me to approach these situations proactively?
- How do I want to see myself in this situation?
- Who do I yearn to be?
- What is the ideal outcome of these situations?

Once you've identified the resistance and how you ideally want to be around it, make a plan that honors progress over perfection. What is one thing you can do today that will move you closer to your chosen outcome? How can you take a step forward and become more Unleashed in this area of your life? How can you lead yourself and be accountable to your values and vision?

PROGRESS WILL ALWAYS MOVE YOU FORWARD

There's no such thing as negative progress. Every step you take is one step closer to where you're going.

But what happens when you get stuck—like, *really* stuck, to the point where "just getting started" is no longer an option? When that happens, it's likely time for a transformation—not just a step forward, but an opening to a new awareness that has the potential to permanently shift how you show up and engage with life.

Buckle up, baby, because we're going there.

CHAPTER 9

BADASSES UNITE

I once made an investment to take part in a yearlong coaching container and mastermind that promised to teach us (the participants) how to grow multiple six- and seven-figure coaching businesses by optimizing digital marketing and building a team to support those efforts.

The package also included a few in-person masterminds, which was the main reason I signed up. I craved a community of driven, authentic individuals who were on a similar path to mine.

The in-person mastermind format was something known as "hot seats." Each person would receive thirty minutes of laser coaching from the lead coach and her support staff in the "hot seat" at the front of the room. While this style of coaching can sound scary, it can be very empowering and effective when facilitated with care, attention, and clear ground rules by a guide who is strong in their own authentic power.

In this case, however, none of the above were true.

From the hot seat, one woman I respected shared how she was struggling with the dynamic her increased success was creating in her marriage. She wanted advice on how to balance her business with expectations in her household, and feared that her financial success was emasculating her partner.

For the next thirty minutes, I sat in utter shock as our coaches (you know, the ones we'd paid thousands of dollars to teach us how to market our business authentically in the online space) explained that "it's our job as women to make our man feel in power." They talked about how to "make him feel good," and how not to "take away success from him."

Their advice? "Don't talk too much about business with your partner. That's not what he wants from you. Be a wife. Dress up sexy for him. Make him feel wanted. Mix it up and keep it fun, so he stays on his toes." The lead coach even went so far as to recommend websites where we could shop for sexy lingerie and costumes.

Now, you may or may not agree with the advice given (I certainly didn't!), but the issue wasn't the advice itself or even the subject matter, although that was far outside the scope of what the mastermind was about. The issue for me was that the advice didn't take into account what the client in the hot seat felt about the situation.

I could feel the dissonance deep in my body. What about supporting the client to uncover what she wanted the relationship dynamic to look and feel like? What about helping her uncover her truth, and shift any old beliefs that were holding her back? What about ... you know, actual *coaching?*

Even more shocking to me than the coaches' behavior was that many of the women in the room—including the cringing CEO in the "hot seat"—were nodding their heads in agreement. Like this was exactly what they thought they needed to hear, even if they didn't feel right about it on the inside.

And so, despite every cell in my body yearning to stand up and scream, *"You don't have to make yourself smaller for anyone!"* I kept quiet. I made myself smaller, too.

Clearly, this was not the community of Unleashed women I'd thought I was signing up for. This was a group that had bought into the patriarchal norm of "Marriage is husband plus wife, and wife serves husband." (Not that there's anything wrong with that if it brings you and your partner authentic joy—but I don't believe in telling *any* woman that there's one prescribed path for how all women are supposed to be. Never mind how exclusionary the whole model is to anyone who doesn't have a traditional husband/wife partnership!)

What was even worse, though, was that I knew, even as my thoughts whirled and my body sweated, that I was complicit in that narrative simply by staying to participate. My presence implied my agreement that this coaching was okay. I wish I could say that I never went back. But I finished out the year, because I was still grappling with my own self-doubt within that program, and questioning if there was something wrong with me for not agreeing with the women at the front of the room. In the end, I did learn some new and useful strategies, but I never recovered my sense of trust for and alignment with the coach. And when it was my turn in the hot seat, I was cautious about asking for guidance about anything vulnerable, personal, or near to my heart.

THE POWER OF COMMUNITY

Some of my best friends are the women I studied abroad with in Kenya.

There's something about spending a year together where everyone has something stolen, unknowingly breaks some important cultural taboo, and poops their pants at least once (because, new foods and water), that bonds you together like nothing else.

A few years after we all graduated, two of those girl-friends, Jessie and Nicole, were visiting. They had plans to go to Concerts on the Square, a staple summer event in my college town. The concert series was an elegant event taking place on the lawn of the capitol building. People would bring their own cheese, wine, and hors d'oeuvres to enjoy an evening of classical music.

On the night of the concert, my band just happened to be playing a gig at a dive bar a few blocks down the street from the square. Of course, I eagerly invited Jessie and Nicole to join us, since they'd never seen my band play before.

Despite having zero experience with (or interest in) metal music, they enthusiastically agreed. And they showed up in full effect, complete with fancy white blouses and khaki pants.

The three of us had experienced culture shock while studying in Kenya. In its own way, this was just as jarring. They stood out amongst the metalheads like—well, like the upscale, classical-music-loving women they were. For a moment, I had no idea how this was all going to go down.

But, as I should have known from the start, none of it mattered. Despite the fact that they would never have listened to metal if they didn't know me, they got right out on the dance floor. They headbanged like champs and screamed my name at the tops of their lungs. To this day, I can still see them rocking to the beat, arms in the air, hair flying as they owned their office-glam like absolute badasses.

This is what true friends will do for you. Even if they don't fully understand your Unleashed-ness, they will show up and dance and scream your name because they love to watch you shine.

The truth is, the more Unleashed you become, the more you will have to dig to find truly aligned people and communities. This isn't because there are no Unleashed people in the world—there are lots of us!—but because when you understand your values and boundaries, and get clear on what's right for you and what isn't, anything and anyone that's not a match for you will feel icky.

As an Unleashed individual, you will still be a unique person inside your chosen communities, with your own ways of doing things and seeing the world. The goal isn't to find people who agree with you about everything (if you do find a community like that, run the other way, because it's a cult!). Instead, it's to find a community with a *shared philosophy* and a unifying set of values—an ecosystem where you are nurtured, and where your uniqueness feeds the whole. That way, you can find a common ground of mutual respect with those around you even when you disagree about hot-button issues.

"BEING UNLEASHED
DOESN'T MEAN
NOT GIVING A FUCK
ABOUT WHAT PEOPLE
THINK. YOU DIDN'T
STOP BEING HUMAN.
IT JUST MEANS
ONLY GIVING A FUCK
ABOUT WHAT THE
RIGHT PEOPLE THINK."

Sadly, however, not all communities are built with this intention. Some gardens—as I found out the hard way in those early coaching groups—are meant to grow only one type of flower.

You can find community in many places—from spiritual groups to exercise clubs, local libraries to giant conventions, old friends to Facebook friend groups, highly-choreographed networking sessions to random coffeehouse encounters. But, some of the best and most aligned communities I've found have been in paid spaces.

In the entrepreneurial world, paid communities are extremely common. You are paying someone (or a group of someones) to organize and hold a container for a specific purpose. People are financially invested, so they're committed, and they are more likely to hold themselves to that commitment. And they have shown, through their decision to invest, that they are ready to uplevel in whatever way the community is intended to support.

In a paid community, everyone is asking similar questions. More, they aren't afraid to bring those questions, because the whole point of the group is to get them answered. While you will find people you love in these spaces, it's not the same as hanging out with friends— because, unlike with friends, where it's important that things are mutually balanced and beneficial, in a paid community you are paying for support with the expectation of receiving it. It's a different type of exchange.

You have reached a point where you are owning your authenticity. You have uncovered your previous programming to find your truth. You've unlocked your authenticity.

Now, your Unleashed self has come out to play—and you deserve a community that supports, validates, and absolutely adores you for who you are, and who you are becoming.

So, how do you find those people?

First, lean into your values and guiding principles. They will never steer you wrong.

Second, stop judging yourself for wanting to be seen, heard, and valued.

When I joined that first coaching group, I really wanted someone to pat me on the shoulder and say, "Wow, Amber! You're doing an awesome job. Now, how can we help you do this in a way that's even more *you*?" Instead, I ended up judging myself for once again desiring validation but not receiving it.

I used to say to myself: "If you're so empowered, Am, you wouldn't be trying to prove yourself to them or seeking validation." This kept me stuck in a loop of self-judgment and shame, to the point where I started thinking, "Maybe they're doing it the right way, and I'm in the wrong."

(Are you beginning to see a theme here? Yup. Imposter syndrome!)

Since that time, I've learned that healthy validation is valuable and powerful. It allows you to be seen and heard, and creates the safety for you to be open and vulnerable in a space so you can release what no longer serves you, heal it, and move past it. But seeking validation in an unhealthy way, from unaligned people, can harm more than it helps.

I may not have gotten the validation I was looking for in that first coaching group, but I did learn a valuable lesson about what I actually wanted and needed from a mentor. Instead of asking, "Will this program help me make more money," or, "Will this coach teach me this strategy?" my questions became, "Does this person align with my core values and guiding principles? Do they want the same things for me that I want for myself? Do they want what I want for the collective?"

Here's the truth. Being Unleashed doesn't mean not giving a fuck about what people think. You didn't stop being human. It just means only giving a fuck about what the *right* people think. So make sure that you're hanging out with as many of the right people *for you* as you can find, and have fun exploring who you are with them.

And hey, if you can't find a community of badasses who share your values and guiding principles and are ready to live Unleashed alongside you ... well, you can always create your own, or consider joining mine.

THE BIRTH OF SOUL SEED

In January of 2020, we were approaching the five-year mark in my business Strategic Partners Marketing. By this point my business had evolved, and while I technically had one business, I had two brands within it: the company itself, Strategic Partners Marketing, which is the brand strategy and marketing agency I'd founded when I left my job and jumped into the unknown, and within that business was a product line called Impact Academy where I offered transformational coaching, speaking, and retreats. I didn't like how split I felt between the two sides of my business. They shared an overarching mission to help people live and lead authentically and to help conscious businesses to be more successful, but services on the marketing agency side were a bit more agency-like, and the services on the coaching side were more spiritual, personal development, and coaching-like.

At the time, I was feeling extremely stuck around how to bring those two sides of the business into alignment. I had a limiting belief that they were too different, and I feared we'd lose clients if we merged the messaging and vision all into one. I worried that our more traditional marketing clients would think we were too "woo"—even though the "woo" is the core foundation to all conscious business success. I began to think that maybe I should sell the agency so that I could then focus on growing the side of the business that was focused on personal development and transformation.

Eventually, I decided the best thing to do was the "usual" route: put Strategic Partners Marketing on the market and see if someone would acquire it, thus validating all my years of hard work and freeing me up to do what my soul was calling for, which was something beyond "just marketing." Of course, the Universe delivered. I hadn't even put my business out there for sale when a company reached out to me and initiated discussions about possibly acquiring my agency.

As conversations progressed with this group, I started to feel torn. My logical mind was saying, "You have to sell or merge your business with another traditional marketing firm so you don't lose all the brand value you've built." For a small team, we'd carved a remarkable niche for ourselves in the brand and marketing space. We cleared benchmarks most small businesses never reach, and I was really proud of that. How could I just rebrand and become something new, or close up shop and walk away because I was aligned with a new vision?

I felt very emotional and torn. I worried about losing clients, revenue, and my team if I made too dramatic a change. But I also knew that staying the way things were wasn't going to solve anything. I didn't love having a brand that felt split. By this point in my growth, I had started trusting my intuition first and foremost, and so I pressed pause, and listened.

This isn't a time for progress over perfection, my intuition whispered. *This is a radical shift, and you need to be present to it.*

I knew that something new was meant to come forth, and I didn't want to walk that journey on my own. I'd been stuck in that loop for the past few years already as these two sides of my business were growing separately from each other—which was what had gotten me into this mess in the first place. I was tired of being stuck. It was time to receive guidance and find an aligned coach and community to help me process the massive shift that was taking place in my business, and within me.

About a year before, I'd been introduced to a woman named Darla LeDoux, who coaches transformational leaders.

I signed up for private coaching with Darla—and while I only had a fuzzy idea about what I would actually receive from it, intuitively it felt right. So, in a complete state of surrender and trust, and with a commitment to do whatever was necessary to overcome the discomfort of my current stuckness and finally come to a decision about whether to keep or sell or rebrand my business, I stepped in.

Not long after I started working with Darla, my questions surrounding a business sale answered themselves. After several exploratory conversations with potential buyers, I realized that, if my business was acquired, it would require me going along with it for a few years. When I considered the time and energy I'd spend working in the new company and creating someone else's brand and culture, I realized it wasn't worth it. I could just invest that time and energy into birthing forward a new vision for my own business. Ultimately, I decided not to sell and instead committed to trusting the transformation that was unfolding.

What we were offering clients went well beyond marketing. It was transformational brand strategy and personal coaching that helped people transform at a soul level and leverage their personal truth as a path to freedom in both their businesses and their lives. We also offered marketing services—but most of our clients only graduated to that phase after doing the initial transformation work. Over the years we had found that, in order for businesses to be successful in marketing, they needed a solid brand strategy and self-alignment in place. In many ways, we had *already* evolved into a transformation agency. But our business name at the time, our branding, and some of the marketing language our team was speaking wasn't fully aligned to the vision I had for what we could become. It was like I had evolved a few steps ahead of the rest of my company—which made sense, considering how much work I'd done to take myself off the leash in my life over the last five years. Now, it was time to bring all of it into alignment, and for me to become the Unleashed leader that I was capable of being.

All this happened because I entered into coaching with the simple intention of "getting clear on what comes next."

This is one of my favorite stories to share about my business journey because it's an example of a time that I trusted my inner knowing even when my logical mind didn't understand. So many of us miss great opportunities to bring ourselves deeper into alignment and joy because we are looking for logical explanations. We want to know what tangible thing we are going to get from an investment of time, money, or energy. At some stages of our growth, this tactic will make sense—but when we reach a critical plateau, our answers won't come from tactics. They will only ever come from transformation.

At the time that I invested in coaching for myself, there were a lot of reasons why I could have logically opted out. The Covid-19 pandemic had just started. I was stressed, busy, and dealing with clients paralyzed by their own fear, a huge drop in revenues, and loads of uncertainty.

Ironically, though, those were all reasons why I actually *needed* coaching and support more than ever. Just as this was why my clients needed my support more than ever.

The crazier things got, the more I benefited from the safety of the coaching container. More, it was a space created for me to get grounded in my knowing and in my vision for leadership. Despite the challenges, 2020 was one of our biggest company growth years—and one of the biggest years for many of our clients too.

During this time, I also came to understand my unique Human Design. For the first time, I understood that my deep feelings are part of my unique design, and that they are a superpower as long as I engage them in a way that is aligned to my unique energy and decision-making author-ity. My gifts include strategy and expansion—I can intui-tively see a big vision and understand the strategic steps to get there—combined with the ability to feel soul-truth. You might say I *feel* energy. I *feel* when someone says one thing and means something else—even if they don't consciously understand it themselves. I feel what and where people's limiting beliefs and conditioning are. This knowingness got me in all kinds of trouble as a kid, when I would call out the adults in my family for being "full of it"—and so I learned to shut it down. Being able to deeply examine this and test it out in a judgment-free zone was empowering.

In my coaching, it was about holding me in my energy. I was already expert at business strategy; I wasn't there to get help with what I already mastered. Instead, I was there to receive whatever was ready to come through for my next stage of the journey—and I refused to be gaslit any longer by my own self-doubt.

Staying in that place of tuning into my body, my energy, and feelings week after week was *so* uncomfortable, because

"YOUR UNLEASHED LIFE IS A MISSION TO BECOME ALL OF WHO YOU ARE. NOTHING MORE, NOTHING LESS."

my programming wanted to jump to the strategic doing. The container was 100 percent about getting me present to my own energy. Only then could I actually invite an epic, next-level vision for my business.

That vision came through with the creation of Soul Seed, the brand born from my soul. As soon as I thought up Soul Seed, I knew it was *it*. It was the first time in five years that I felt fully aligned with my business. I declared that Soul Seed's mission was global healing, and that everything I did from that point forward would be aligned to elevating consciousness. We would do this through a multi-pronged ecosystem with several businesses and product lines that share that mission.

The vision seemed to pour out of me. I drew up the ecosystem for what Soul Seed is and represents, with Soul Seed as the "mother-brand," and multiple specific brands within that energy.

Today within Soul Seed are three businesses: Soul Seed Strategy, where we provide transformational brand strategy, marketing, and coaching to help elevate conscious leaders and companies. Soul Seed CBD, where my husband and family and I grow hemp and support conscious living with plant-based natural wellness products for visionaries and creators. And my third business is my personal brand: Amber Swenor, heart-centered badass, frontwoman, and visionary strategist, where I offer coaching, consulting, retreats, and of course, speaking on stages.

When I gave life to this vision, for the first time in my life I felt completely at clarity and peace with my business name, brand, vision, vibe, purpose. Within weeks of making the decision to rebrand and become Soul Seed (but before the actual rebrand even happened), we began attracting a new, upleveled type of conscious leader client—the exact clients I had deeply visualized and felt us serving!

Until I actually stepped in and did the work, I couldn't have known that Soul Seed would be the result. All I knew was what I felt, and I decided to trust it. My brand is the latest and greatest manifestation of my Unleashed life to date.

And the best part? Now that I understand what the next level of "Unleashed" looks like for me, I am even more equipped to guide my clients in their transformational journeys. I am potently present in my sessions, able to energetically pick up on things that I may not have noticed before. This leads my clients to more profound insights and awarenesses that we can then work with to elevate their brands. Results that once took months are happening for some clients in a matter of weeks, or days—all because I am no longer holding back pieces of myself out of misplaced fear or self-doubt. Instead, I'm fully engaged with my gifts in my zone of genius, for the benefit of everyone.

Living Unleashed (in life and business) might be the greatest gift you can give yourself. But it's also a gift for others.

YOU WILL WALK ALONE, BUT YOU'RE NEVER ALONE

As an Unleashed visionary, you are being called to walk a path that few have traveled. You are called to this—but you won't know what it looks like until you actually do it.

I never would have guessed, during those years as a struggling waitress in college, a pageant reject, or a small-town metalhead, that I would be where I am today. If you had told me that I'd be opening for epic rock and metal bands, or that I'd have my own dedicated fan base, or that I'd be running a multi-tiered soul-centric company focused on upleveling consciousness through business, I would have laughed in disbelief. And yet, this is what "Unleashed" looks like for me, and I wouldn't have it any other way. It's so perfectly aligned with who I've always known myself to be.

When you are called forward, you must go. Follow the thread of your inner knowing. Do it for *you*. Don't worry if no one follows you right away—they will, because they, too, want to become Unleashed. When you have walked into your own truth, you become magnetic in a way that is irreplicable.

It may take some time for you to find your people, or for them to find you. Keep going. There were a handful of people at our first shitty gigs. Today, we play for hundreds at epic lineups and festivals. And out there, in the crowd, are that same handful of early believers, along with all the new people who have joined our family along the way.

The same has happened in my business life. Years ago, I felt like a leashed unicorn in some of those coaching and networking spaces. Now, I've both found and created my own communities that I can lean into with trust, and support through my gifts.

Your Unleashed life is a mission to become all of who you are. Nothing more, nothing less. But although no one on the planet will ever be exactly like you, you don't have to walk the path alone. Along the way, you will meet those true believers—those who will show up for you even where there's no "proof" yet of your greatness. Remember that you are a lighthouse for them, showing the way—and that they believe in you because they see that light, even when you can't.

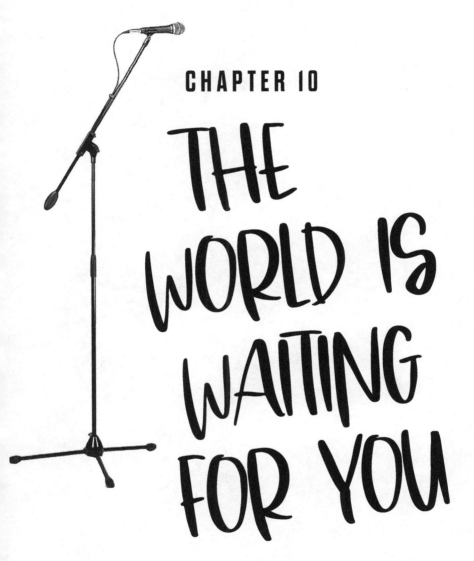

CHAPTER 10

THE WORLD IS WAITING FOR YOU

"Amber, your eyes light up when you talk about this 'Soul Seed' thing."

It was 2018, and I was at lunch with one of my dear friends and mentors, the late Amy Gannon. I was still at the beginning stages of the dilemma I shared with you in Chapter 9—choosing between the two emerging sides of my business and moving from pure marketing to coaching and transformational strategy.

I was explaining to Amy about all the things I needed to "check off the list," and "have in order," in my agency before I could spend more time actually following through on my soul-work. (Otherwise know as procrastinating and delaying my purpose.)

Amy listened with an amused smile. Eventually, she said, "Why can't you just do all of this now?"

The question stopped me in my tracks. "Why *can't* I do that now?" I wondered aloud.

Every answer that came to mind was nothing more than an excuse born of fear. *Well, I can't just pivot to coaching, what will our agency clients think? I have staff. If I start focusing too much on coaching and marketing clients drop off, how will I pay everyone on the team?* But the true reason—the one rooted in truth—was simply that I wasn't clear yet about how I wanted my business to evolve, and so I was doubting myself.

Amy didn't doubt me. She didn't question whether I *could* do what I was envisioning. She merely wondered why I was *choosing not to*.

Her support and belief in me was a catalyst. Through our conversation, I became braver in taking action on my desires. I stopped pushing things to someday and started allowing myself to act on them, beginning the biggest expansion in my life thus far: moving from "safe" work into soul-work.

I hope that you also have someone in your life who will lovingly hold you in your truth when your inner bullshit meter is ding-ding-dinging off the charts. Someone who will inspire you to go to a deeper level of truth, where you release fear and muster the courage to go for what you already know you are meant to do.

Amy was that person for me. She was unapologetic. A total badass powerhouse. Her mission (through Doyenne, an organization that she co-founded) was to create a more inclusive entrepreneurial ecosystem for women and people of color, and she was totally willing to hit on people's nerves if that was what it took to advance the mission. She also held the entrepreneurs and visionaries in her community lovingly, safely, and in a way that made all of us feel that we could truly do anything.

Amy's question, "Why can't you just do all of this now?" was simple, but powerful. It reminded me that I had a choice, even when I didn't have clarity. And so, I took her encouragement and combined it with everything I've shared with you in this book. I embraced progress over perfection. I chose joy over judgment. And, little by little, I kept playing in the energy of this new version of me, and allowing this new expression to be visible in my business and leadership.

I began offering more coaching webinars and work-shops to "sound check" my ideas. I didn't focus on how many people attended—and sometimes only a handful showed up. I just focused on helping one person at a time. And with each new experiment, I made my soul voice louder than my imposter voice. I shared my message even when I had no idea whether or not it was being received, or if it was making a difference.

I also made it a practice to move forward despite what my agency clients might think. This didn't affect their work with me, I reminded myself. I wasn't dropping any balls just because I was playing in this new space. And even while I was actively practicing progress over per-fection, I attracted in a new group of aligned people who were receiving guidance and experiencing growth—many of whom were the same clients whose transformational stories I've shared in this book.

It took a solid two years of playing in that "messy mid-dle" space before I could finally see all the pieces of the future vision I laid out in that conversation with Amy—but it didn't matter. What counted was that I was on my way.

The messy middle. The angsty unknown. The place where your future seems like nothing more than a shadow on the horizon, calling you forward. The path isn't clear. Only when you pause and look back can you actually con-nect the dots and see why you came this way.

Maybe you're there now. Maybe you're teetering on the border. Maybe your Unleashed future is nothing more than a smudge on the horizon of your current lifescape. It's okay.

Just take a step. And another. You are living your journey and writing your story as we speak. You'll get there.

THE UNLEASHED RIPPLE

In 2019, I attended a retreat with Amy. I shared about the steps I was taking toward my vision and how I was navigating the still-shifting currents in my business.

"Amber," Amy said, holding my eyes with hers. "People will follow you wherever you go."

In that moment, I felt seen. It wasn't what I was creating that was important. It wasn't what I was doing or not doing in my business. The X-factor, the non-negotiable piece of the whole puzzle, wasn't some task list or strategy. It was *me*.

I had been presenting as a total badass for years, but that day, Amy saw within me the visionary leader I was fully capable of being but hadn't yet allowed to be fully visible.

That was one of the last times I saw Amy. Three months later, a few days before the turn of the year, she passed away with her young daughter in a tragic helicopter accident.

Her death shook all of us who had known her. She was a beacon in our community, a bright light that we weren't prepared to lose, let alone so soon. But her light lives on through the thousands of entrepreneurs she impacted— and they in turn are impacting millions of lives. The impact of her Unleashed life ripples through all of us.

This is why, when you are called, you must go.

Your Unleashing is all about you—but it's also far, far bigger than you.

We find our way to freedom through our personal truth, our values, our actions, and our communities. We find our way by finding ourselves. We do the work. And then, we show the way to others.

THE RISE OF THE UNLEASHED VISIONARY

Years ago, while doing market research, I posted a question to my social channels:

"What does 'Heart-Centered Leadership' mean to you?"

There were a variety of responses, most of which were positive and felt aligned with my personal perception. And then, there were a few like, "It means you cry a lot. You're too emotional. You can't handle business and life."

As we've discovered together in this book, living Unleashed means leaning into your inner wisdom, values, and guiding principles, and feeling your feelings. Without this sensitivity, your "logical" (read: conditioned) mind will take over and keep you trapped in a maze of "shoulds."

But even beyond its implications for exploring and living your personal truth, "heart-centeredness" is a strength—one I beg you not to discount.

You came to this world with love in you. Your sensitivity, your empathy, your deep, powerful feelings? Those can't be taught. They are strengths, not weaknesses. You know what *can* be taught? Bookkeeping. Marketing. Management. Logic and rational debate.

Guess which skill set is more powerful for visionary leadership?

You are being called to live Unleashed because you are, ultimately, meant to lead. Even if you don't see leadership (in business or otherwise) as part of your path right now, I'm confident that it will find you in the future. Because when you become Unleashed, people will follow wherever you go.

This world is waiting for you to rise.

An Unleashed person understands how to empower others to expand. They understand that a brand, or a family, or a community, is strengthened just as much by what it does or says internally as by how it performs externally. They understand that whole people who are living freely in their personal truth create outstanding results in both business and relationships. They understand that, for anyone to do their best, they have to *be* their best.

Unleashed leaders are the future. And whether you're leading a company, a community, a family, a classroom, or simply leading yourself, it's high time you embrace this part of you.

COMING HOME TO YOU

Dogs. Africa. Rock-n-roll.

These are some of my earliest truths. I never could have imagined, back in my small hometown, that they would take me around the world, onto big stages under bright lights, and right back around into a deeper alignment with the true me.

I'm still that same girl. Wearing pleather and earmuffs in the summer. Belting "Heartbreaker" in seven-inch platforms in a beauty pageant. Covered in glitter and roaring into a mic. Jumping for joy on my dumpster mattress. But now, freed from the chains of my conditioning, powered by intuition, and deeply connected to the truth and freedom that's been in my soul all along, just waiting to be Unleashed.

Let yourself come home to your truth, amplified with abundance. Let the smog of others' expectations clear. Switch off the filter of imposter syndrome. Live in the joy of the present while creating your most amazing future.

Welcome home to *you*, my gorgeous, badass, Unleashed friend.

"THE WORLD
IS WAITING
FOR YOU
TO RISE."

RESOURCES

For these book-related resources and more, visit
www.amber-swenor.com/resources

BUSINESS ALIGNMENT ASSESSMENT (ONLINE QUIZ/ASSESSMENT)

To holistically align your business with your purpose, take
the business alignment assessment (this aligns energy +
mindset + strategy). A holistic business alignment assessment to assess 7 key areas of your business and see where
your greatest assets and gaps are.

5 STEPS TO BUILD YOUR BRAND (EMAIL SERIES)

The first 5 steps to grow a values-aligned brand, that is
aligned to your profit, purpose, and positioning.

UNCOVER YOUR DREAMS & UNLEASH YOUR IMPACT (A GUIDED WORK-
BOOK FOR ANYONE AT ANY STAGE IN THE JOURNEY)

Feel a soul nudge to something different? Feeling stuck and
aren't sure how or where to take the next step? Start here.

BOOK RECOMMENDATIONS

The Big Leap: Conquer Your Hidden Fears and Take Your Life to the Next Level by Gay Hendricks

ASSESSMENTS

Clifton StrengthsFinder:
www.gallup.com/cliftonstrengths

Human Design, get your free chart:
www.jovianarchive.com/Get_Your_Chart

Join the Soul Seed network:
A community of visionary change-makers, creators, and heart-centered leaders on a mission to grow businesses through profits rooted in purpose. Visit www.soul-seed.com

CONSULTATIONS

Not sure what your next steps are? Book a consultation with Amber and her team!

Book Amber to speak:
Email: amber@soul-seed.com with your request. Please include the event information, date(s) and requested topics.

For business strategy and marketing consultation visit www.soulseedstrategy.com/consult

For personal coaching consultation visit: www.soulseedstrategy.com/unleashnow

ACKNOWLEDGMENTS

While it's impossible to thank or acknowledge every person who has impacted my life—and, subsequently, this book—there are a few in the journey without whom I'm certain I would not be writing these words today. For that I thank the following humans who have profoundly impacted me.

To Mr. Jerry Ashenbrenner (Mr. A.), my school FFA advisor and agriculture instructor: During these formative years between seventh and twelfth grade—some of the most emotionally gut-wrenching in my journey to true-self-awareness—I was tremendously lucky and grateful to have you as a guide and mentor, like a second father, encouraging me and believing in me, and also putting your foot down with caring reprimand when you saw that I could do better in my decisions. *"Youth don't care how much you know, until they know how much you care,"* was the quote on a sign that hung at the front of your classroom. And you walked that walk every day. You showed me the power in pausing for presence, in shooting the shit with people you liked, and laughing every day. You always made time for me—and for every student that walked through your door—and never tamped down my spirit to make me fit into others' expectations. To this day, I still don't know how you could stand to listen to the same speeches on agriculture, land management, or North American wolf revitalization five hundred times as we timed and honed and perfected them—but you gave your full attention every time. I can still hear you saying, in your deep, one-of-a-kind "Mr. A" voice, "Now, Miss Amber, don't you worry about going over the time a little bit. You've got a winner of a speech here and they need to hear the whole thing!" I guess you had a rebel streak in you, too! And you were right: I didn't marry my high school sweetheart. You always knew our small town couldn't contain me. Although you passed in 2016, I can still imagine you chuckling in amusement at who I've become, because you wouldn't be surprised by any of it. You saw it from the start—long before I could see it for myself. This book is dedicated to your spirit, your heart, and your authentic contribution to the thousands of lives you touched through your work.

To the man who walks beside me every day in all ways— my friend, lover, fellow creator, and music man, Brandon: I love you.

To my mom, Cindy: I get my heart-centeredness from you. Thank you for showing me the power of being kind.

To my dad, David: I get my badass from you. Thank you for creating within me a foundation for authenticity.

To both of my parents, while I know that, sometimes, parenting me may have felt beyond your capabilities, you never stopped doing it. Even Unleashed rockstars need the love of their mom and dad, and I'm grateful to always have not only your love, but your friendship too.

To Titus and Nova, our beloved pups: the days we got you were two of the happiest in my life. I thank you for teaching me that *now* is the only time. You ground me in today, every day.

To my baby brother and bandmate, Davey: thank you for being my friend. You test my patience and have helped me strengthen my boundaries. You're my "twin-flame" sibling. Some days we have brought out the worst in each other, but as we get older, I'm grateful that we are bringing out more of each other's best.

To my team members, past, present, and future: our collective impact wouldn't exist without all of your contributions. Soul Seed wouldn't be what it is today, and I wouldn't be the leader that I am, without you.

To all of our Soul Seed clients, past, current, and future: it's an honor to be in the journey with you, serving, guiding, facilitating, and creating something meaningful together. I've always believed that profits rooted in purpose was possible, and you proved it.

To Darla LeDoux: your guidance was profound in facilitating my steps across the threshold to becoming Unleashed.

To Bryna Haynes and the World Changers Media team: thank you for your expert and caring guidance, for believing in me and my message, and for all the ways you've helped to elevate this book and make it even better.

To the late Amy Gannon: thank you for being a badass. Thank you for believing in me. Thank you for the ways that you taught me how to take a stand for women, and for anti-racism. Thank you for being bold about your beliefs, regardless of what anyone thought about it.

To my amazing, loving, fun, and caring friends and family members who have loved me and supported me, even if you have thought that my ideas and holiday cards are a bit weird (it's true, they are): some of you have known me forever and we ground each other in the ways that only friends and cousins who've grown up together can do (Mel, Cassie, Peggy, Krissy). Some of you saw me standing in my light and your encouragement helped me to trust it and allow it to shine even brighter (Nicole Budeau). And some of you do a mighty fine job of holding me accountable and not buying my bullshit, while loving all of me (Nicole Irungu, Jessie Lerner). Even though you may not be named, to every person I call a friend, I freaking love you and I'm grateful for you.

To everyone who has contributed to the phenomenal work of the Vital Voices Global Partnership: thank you for believing in social impact leaders like me. Vital Voices Global Partnership invests in women leaders solving the world's greatest challenges, from gender-based violence to the climate crisis, economic inequities, and more. Vital Voices are venture catalysts, identifying those leaders with a daring vision for change and partnering with them to make that vision a reality. Since founding in 1997, they've built a network of 20,000 change-makers across 186 countries, who are collectively daring to reimagine a more equitable world for us all. I'm grateful to be a part of this profound network.

Today, I've found a way to be completely me, and it's largely as a result of the people named above, and the dozens of others who I thank every day in spirit, energy, and soul. Just because your name isn't inked on this paper doesn't mean that you are inked any less in my heart.

And so, my last "Thank you!" is to every heart-centered badass, every sensitive soul, every starseed, every visionary, and every human who is finding the spaces in their world where they can be Unleashed. You are bold, even if you aren't loud; you are making your voices heard without drowning out others. You are shining your light without needing others to dim theirs. You are amplifying authenticity every day. Together, we are creating an Unleashed world.

ABOUT THE AUTHOR

As a heart-centered metalhead and transformational brand and business strategist (yes, that's really a thing!) Amber Swenor is passionate about helping humans to live more authentically. In particular, she helps visionary entrepreneurs to grow purpose-driven businesses by uncovering their soul-aligned, values-driven strategy that also aligns their passion, profits, and positioning.

As a young woman, Amber was a natural leader, serving in numerous youth leadership positions in high school and college. Her mantra, "It doesn't matter who you are or where you come from; you can do anything!" empowered her to be the first generation in her family to graduate from high school (as valedictorian), attend college at the University of Wisconsin Madison, and travel around the world in search of authentic, aligned experiences. She worked in Turkmenistan through Winrock International with teachers and students to establish their first-ever agriculture-related youth leadership organization, and spent a year in Kenya studying abroad and interning with the African Women leaders in Agriculture program.

Her experience in sales, marketing, and entrepreneurial positioning in numerous positions empowered her to launch Strategic Partners Marketing in 2015, a Madison, WI-based agency with a mission to help small businesses bring strategic decision-making into their marketing. Since then, the company has evolved, and was rebranded as Soul Seed in 2021, highlighting Amber's mission for elevating conscious leaders and companies through values-based branding. Today, the Soul Seed family of brands includes brand strategy, marketing, and coaching; Soul Seed CBD, which produces home-grown, hemp-based products; and Amber's personal brand as a speaker, coach, and consultant.

Amber believes that "Your personal truth is the path to freedom." She's proud to have been a Vital Voices Global Partnership VVGrow Fellow (2018), as well as a global trainer with Vital Voices. She's also a 2019 Goldman Sachs 10,000 Small Businesses Graduate, and a member and trainer in the entrepreneurial organization Doyenne. Her message around living in greater authenticity while going full-out for your dreams has landed her on world-wide media.

When she's not strategizing with clients, speaking on stages, or getting her hands dirty in the hemp fields, you can find Amber rocking alongside her husband Brandon in their metal band, Morningstar. And, as much as she adores big, bold moves, some of her favorite days are spent snuggled up with a book and her pups, Titus and Nova.

Learn more about Amber's work at
www.Soul-Seed.com and www.Amber-Swenor.com

ABOUT THE PUBLISHER

Founded in 2021 by Bryna Haynes, WorldChangers Media is a boutique publishing company focused on "Ideas for Impact."

We know that great books change lives, topple outdated paradigms, and build movements. Our commitment is to deliver superior-quality transformational nonfiction by, and for, the next generation of thought leaders.

Ready to write and publish your thought leadership book with us? Learn more at www.WorldChangers.Media

CPSIA information can be obtained
at www.ICGtesting.com
Printed in the USA
JSHW062024160822
29345JS00004B/19